WOMAN OF
PURPOSE, POWER
AND PASSION

WOMAN OF PURPOSE, POWER AND PASSION

~ An Anthology of Hope & Direction ~

Compiled by Shanene Higgins
Coauthors
Sherae Bell * Laura Bella
Janie Bess * Berta Jean * Rein Johnson
Michele Mills * Dr. Lakita Long

Dallas, TX

Higgins Publishing Since 2002

Woman of Purpose, Power and Passion
Copyright 2014 – Higgins Publishing

Library of Congress Control Number: 2014906184
First Revised Edition 2022
Pages cm 202 * Includes Index

ISBN: 978-0-981520-24-7 (PB) * 978-1-941580-33-2 (EB)
978-1-941580-00-4 (Journal)

Higgins Publishing logos and marks are service marks of
Higgins Publishing

(REL012040) Religion: Christian Life – Inspirational
(SEL021000) Self-Help: Motivational & Inspirational
(SEL016000) Self-Help: Personal Growth - Happiness

For information about special discounts for bulk purchases, subsidiary, foreign and translations rights & permissions, please contact Higgins Publishing at
sales@higginspublishing.com.

DEDICATION

This book is dedicated to you.
We hope that you will find practical solutions that
help you maximize your purpose in life.

To take notes to reflect upon, scan the QR Code
to purchase a copy of the
Woman of Purpose, Power and Passion Journal.

ISBN#: 9781941580004

TABLE OF CONTENTS

INTRODUCTION

The *Woman of Purpose, Power and Passion Anthology* is a book written to touch the hearts of girls and women around the world. It is the intention of the authors to take readers on a journey through their personal lives that are heart wrenching, life altering, and inspiring. I count it a blessing to be chosen by God to bring this book to the masses for the express mission of igniting the purpose, power, and passion in the hearts of those who desire to reach their full potential in life.

Many obstacles blocked the completion of this book, but regardless of that, we have pushed through tragic occurrences of losing loved ones, being hospitalized, and loosing property and other things of value. However, we refused to give up on this venture, and forged forward to its completion. Thus, we believe that you, the reader, will be forever positively changed by the true-life stories in this book, and that you will be inspired to live the life that you were born to live by God's design. Be blessed and encouraged as you glean from the hearts of women of purpose, power, and passion, and maximize who you are by applying the practical concepts shared though out the pages of this book. Always remember, that He who began a good work in you, will be faithful to complete it!

Shanene Higgins,
Publisher & Author

SHANENE L. HIGGINS

Shanene L. Higgins is the Founder, CEO and Publisher of Higgins Publishing. She is a Best-Selling Author and the Visionary behind *The Woman of Purpose, Power and Passion Empowerment Expo*. Shanene is also the Co-Author of *The Change Your Life, the 90-Day Experience: The Path to Your Destiny* and *The Change Your Life: Perfecting Your Purpose.* Shanene was born in Pensacola, Florida, and moved with her family to California at the tender age of 7. She discovered in high school that she enjoyed creating advertising pieces for her marketing class as well as singing in the garage. She was married at the age of 18 and has two beautiful children. She continued to write and sing before she became a Christian in 1988, after being introduced to Christ by a dear friend that she met at work (The San Francisco Chronicle & Examiner), Donna Taylor. She received Jesus into her heart as her personal Lord and Savior and became active in her church home (Acts Full Gospel). She joined the choir and began ministering in song as well as creating programs to teach during Vacation Bible School.

Her life shifted when she went through a traumatic divorce, her daughter was diagnosed with cancer, and she was forced to retire early from her job. She decided to launch out on faith to start her own graphic design company, Divine Designs, while taking care of her 10-year-old daughter recovering from cancer, and her 8-year-old son; who was the bone marrow donor for her daughter. Four years later, she was faced with yet another challenge when she was diagnosed with Sarcoidosis. Regardless of what the doctors said, her belief in the healing and sustaining power of God, and her tenacity would not let her give up. She developed her graphic design company into a full-fledged publishing company as well as attended and graduated from Jubilee Christian Center Bible College.

She was asked by the Bible College Program Coordinator, Karen Deary, to speak during the graduating class ceremony with over 3,000 in attendance. Immediately following she became the Church Administrator at Global Christian Ministries, where she was mentored by Apostle Irene Huston. Apostle Huston encouraged her to continue her educational pursuits. After receiving a degree in Business Administration from the University of Phoenix, her passion increased for publishing in various forms.

Shanene wrote, sung, produced, and released her first Gospel CD (Imagine) under her Artist name, Shaneen Lavette.

Soon following the release of her CD, she received an Award for "Best Contemporary Christian/Gospel EP" from Akademia Music Awards.

Even though times were difficult as well as financially challenging, both her children are productive adults of society and are a joy to her life. She continues to write, sing, produce and publish.

Her passion to fulfill her purpose of bringing true-life stories to the forefront, in print, through music, and on screen is the driving force behind her tenacity. She strongly believes that regardless of what has happened in the past, anyone can overcome by the blood of the Lamb, and the word of their testimony.

Her passion continues to positively impact the world one life at a time through story, song, and on screen.

Speaking Engagement & Special Event Contact
Information:

Shanene Higgins

Email: pr@higginspublishing.com

Web: higginspublishing.com

CHAPTER ONE

Come Out of the Shadows and Into the Light

> *"God has a plan for you, all wrapped up*
> *in the purpose of you."*
> *—Shanene Higgins*

An excerpt from my upcoming book The Control Factor:

It was a dark day in my life. All I wanted to do was hide in the closet and fade away as if life had no more meaning. At least that is what I felt like doing at the time. Why bother going on any longer? No one needed me anymore. My son had been taken away, and my daughter was growing even more distant. What I had allowed to happen in my own household tore at the very core of the foundation that I had built, and there was no one to hold accountable for my lack of trust in God but myself. So, there I sat on the bathroom floor crying my eyes out until I literally ran out of tears. Laying at the foot of the tub, as if I was a raggedy mat with no purpose.

I didn't know what to do. I was broken and I had no one in the physical realm to turn to. So I cried out with a loud voice, "God I need you, please help me!" Then, I heard a car outside pulling into the driveway. I thought to myself, "Oh

God, don't let him -- the man I had chosen to be my husband -- find me."

So, with every ounce of strength that I had left, I rose to my feet, and slowly walked into my son's bedroom, opened the closet door, stepped inside, and fell to my knees. I prayed, "God, if he comes inside, please don't let him find me."

I heard him open the front door and begin to walk up the stairs. I began to tremble out of sheer terror. Suddenly, there was complete silence; there was nothing, no sound, no walking, no breathing. Then, the closet door slid open! I sat there afraid to move a muscle. But then something strange happened. I didn't look up because if I moved, he would know I was hiding from him. Suddenly, he shut the door. He didn't even see me. I was shocked, but I wasn't crazy enough to move until I heard him leave the house, and I locked the door behind him.

A few minutes later I opened the door and looked out the window. He was gone, but so was my son. I left the house, and headed to the only place I felt God covering my children and me during a time of despair when my daughter was deathly ill in Children's Hospital, in Oakland, CA. I went upstairs and sat in the cafeteria by a window wondering how in the world I got here. I was so distraught that I ended up calling two friends to come and pray with me. When they arrived, they ministered to me and encouraged me to depend on God, and to not beat myself up.

Right when they were getting ready to leave, we all stood up. That's when it happened. A gentleman who was on staff at the hospital walked over to the piano and began playing, "Now Behold the Lamb."

I broke into tears right there in the cafeteria because the gift to write and to sing had been smothered and stifled as a direct result of my false representation of me. But God still came to visit me in that cafeteria through the gift of music to touch my heart. I was beside myself. He appeared during one of the most trying times of my life even though I had decided to marry a man without even asking Him first for His approval.

What I am about to share with you is extremely sensitive, but deliverance doesn't come by covering up the challenges, realities, and sins of our past. So here goes.

I did not have a grasp on who I was. I always hid behind the gifts, talents, and confidence of others. I would continue to push them to the forefront while I cowardly stood in the background. I did not have the confidence to be in the front. I thought the folks in the front had everything, so I would stay in my lane *in the back*.

It made perfect sense to me because they had charisma, style, and the attention of the crowd practically everywhere they went. They looked good no matter what they wore. The words they spoke were always eloquent. It seemed as if they were never without a loss for words. You wouldn't find them stumbling over their words or losing their train of thought. Oh, how I aspired to be like them, but I wasn't, so I hid.

I hid in the shadows in hopes of never being pushed into the light. That's right, I purposely refused to be who I knew God had chosen me to be; perfectly and visibly flawed. Not wanting to be seen for what I felt was inferior, to what I believed to be perfection.

I reminded myself of a well-known man in the Bible. He wanted to hide from his calling. Matter of fact, he didn't even want to do what God had called him to do at all. He made excuse after excuse, but he couldn't get out of what he was chosen to do. He did not have the confidence to step into who God said he was. He tended to look at his weakness, as so many of us do. I really had it bad. The man was chosen to deliver the children of Israel out of bondage, but he didn't see himself that way, even though God chose him. But just like Moses, we will all have come face-to-face with our purpose, and we will have to decide as to whether we want to continue to hide in the shadows or come into full view.

Will it be easy? Maybe, maybe not! But everyone is challenged in some way or another, which is a good thing because it requires us to put our trust in God to complete what He has started in us. However, there will be bumps along the road that will cause us to second guess even our own decisions. Like the bump in the road that I had with the husband I chose. I thought I would be able to hide behind him for the rest of my life. He was charismatic, handsome, intelligent, gifted and had animal attraction in spades. I remember the first time that I saw him. It feels like it was just yesterday. I became him in every sense of the word. I completely disappeared into who he was and became who he wanted me to be. Because I did not value who I was, it was easy for me to fade into the fabric of his very being as if I were sewn into the seams of his flesh. I hid behind him because I didn't want to be seen by him. I felt that if he really knew me, he wouldn't love me.

You see, I had a sense of rejection that had nothing to do with him. My biological father abandoned me. I didn't even know what he looked like until I was nine years old, which caused me to never feel totally accepted and loved by any man. The first man that I loved with all my heart ended up leaving me and going away to college, never to return, and my heart was broken into a million little shattered pieces. I was devastated, dehydrated, and literally sick for months. I got down to 86 pounds and my grandmother had to feed me with broth because I couldn't keep anything down.

I felt that I couldn't show the real me to my husband because he might leave me. It was easier for me to act like the perfect woman rather than to be the perfect woman. So I became an illusion of who he thought I was. I didn't see it then as a lie, but it was. I lied to him, and I lied to myself. What I did was nothing short of a boldfaced lie to cover up the truth of a hurting heart that wanted to be loved unconditionally. But I was afraid to be me. So how could I share myself with the husband of my choice for the rest of my life when I was so broken from my first love, and a father who I had no relationship with…

My marriage was the beginning of the completion of the breaking of me. Even though I was a Christian, I had a lot to learn about depending on and trusting God completely, and not making a man into an idol. When I decided to do whatever the husband of my choice told me to do instead of listening to the voice of God, it was one the worst mistakes that I had ever made. His voice carried more weight than God because he had managed to instill fear in me to the point of death, and I was too afraid to stand up for myself.

When he asked me for anything, my answer was a resounding yes. I was weak when it came to him, and I had not even one ounce of courage. He had me right where he wanted me and he controlled me like the hands of a clock. But the fear of men didn't start with him. I remember an incident when I went to visit my father when I was around

6

nine years old. I hammered some nails into the wall to make a self-made lock to keep my brothers out of my room. When my father found out, he picked me up and took me to the fire extinguisher chute and placed my head inside the trap door facing downward. All I could see was the fire below as he dangled me by my feet. I was terrified that he would let me go. I never wanted to see him again after that. As soon as I got a chance, I called my mom and told her that I wanted to come home. That was the beginning of my relationship with fear.

When I came to California from New York, I thought I would be safe. But things quickly turned when I went to visit a relative. His wife was sleeping in one room, and no one else was in the house but me. Then he called me to the back room. I ran to him to see what he wanted. He reached out and grabbed me.

Fear came again, as he pressed up against and refused to let me go. I pleaded for him to let me go, but he didn't listen. Imagine a nine-year-old girl being constrained and pressured by a grown man that was nearly fifty-years-old. But not just any man, a family member in whom I had grown to trust who tricked me into submission by force. That's when the spirit of fear took a grip on me that would take the power of God to shake off. But that was a long time coming.

The more time that the husband of my choice and I spent together, the more I became his puppet on a string. He controlled everything that I did, from the clothes that I wore, to the friends that I had, and the family that I lost. One day we were out running errands and he pulled off an exit on the freeway and stopped the car. He looked at me and said, "If I give you a ring right now, will you marry me?" I had prayed for a sign, and I believed for a moment that was it! But I wasn't quite convinced, and I was too afraid to say no. So just like any other thing that he asked me, my answer was a resounding yes. But that's not the only reason why I said yes. I said yes to him based on his outer appearance and his authoritative presence.

I liked the way he could command a room. Not to mention how good he looked in one black suit with a sleek pair of pants that hugged him like a nicely fit pair of gloves. It didn't hurt that he was always well groomed from head to toe, and always dressed to the nines. His charming personality that lit up the entire room was the icing on the cake. I was attracted to his charismatic nature and ability to charm anyone he came across, including me to the point of denial to his controlling nature.

He knew exactly how to control me through giving me what I wanted through the words that he spoke, and the smoothness of his tongue. I was so hooked on how he made me feel that I didn't see the trap that I had set for myself. But deep down inside I knew that I was disappointing God, and something had to change. But my mind and my flesh were so wrapped up in the feeling of being superficially loved, that it would literally take the hand of God to open my eyes.

At this point I should have been on my face seeking God's forgiveness, but that was the farthest thing from my mind. I had been single for ten years, and I was more than ready to be married with all the perks. Unfortunately, I was too ready, and my flesh got the best of me repeatedly. I didn't know myself like I thought I did. I put myself in a position of temptation and you guessed it, temptation won. I thought I was strong enough to be in his presence for hours on end and not fall into sin.

That goes to show you that I was full of myself, thinking that I was stronger than my flesh, after not having sex for three thousand five hundred and twenty days! Really, talk about being puffed up. I found out that if you put yourself into situations with someone that knows how to push your buttons, heartbreak would follow sooner or later. Unfortunately, when I married the husband of my choice, the sooner came like a thief in the night taking every ounce of dignity I had left. My decision to marry him was a recipe for disaster; especially sense he hardly even knew my kids, who he would often refer to as "your kids." He continually let me know that he didn't care about them like he did his own children.

The process of becoming a blended family was a nightmare that wouldn't end. He was brought up in a time when you only tell a child once to do something, and that's it. That is fine and good but there must be balance in everything. Unfortunately, there wasn't balance in his controlling nature. We never knew what was going to happen next. Even though he was somewhat lenient on my daughter, he was extremely rigid when it came to my son to the point of being an over-the-top disciplinarian. He had a spirit of rage that couldn't be reckoned with by most anyone.

He never got physical with me but his voice cut like a knife, and the look in his eyes reflected that of pure rage when something did not go his way. He would go from zero to sixty in two seconds flat so I dared not rattle his cage. I walked around the house on eggshells. But it didn't matter with him; anything would set him off, especially when it came to the kids. So I lived in a state of fear to keep the peace in the house. No one should have to live like that! It's not natural. God does not intend for us to live in fear, especially not in fear of our mates.

But now the cousins of fear joined in: manipulation, control and anger, reared their ugly heads and took a seat as they collectively joined together as new tenants on our apartment lease. Unfortunately, I would have to deal with them one-by-one through a myriad of events that would cause me to face the reality head on.

I had gotten myself into a marriage without seeking God, and now I was facing the consequences of pretending to be someone that I was not. I was miserable.

I wanted to hide in the beginning of the relationship because it was easy hiding behind his personality, but now, being hidden was killing my spirit. The nails in my casket were being sealed day-by-day as he continually floated from one religion to another; finally becoming a Mormon Priest! That's right, I was married to the first African American Mormon Priest that I knew of, and that my dear was the *last straw*. In no way do I condone divorce because God hates it. But when your mate leaves you, forsakes God, and tries to coerce you to do the same, that's a wrap!

I was in so deep that I couldn't get out on my own. I needed a deliverer. I had no idea that my deliverer would be my own son running away from home. I found out later that he had run right to his biological father's house. The time of not knowing where he was, was the single act that struck something so deeply hidden in me that I cried out to God for my very life. That is when God showed me my own lost reflection in the mirror in my bathroom at three o'clock in the morning. I cried so hard and so long, that I could barely see. I felt like I was about to lose my mind when God showed me that I did not love Him as much as I thought I did. When he showed me with clarity that I had chosen to satisfy my own flesh and obey a man who did not put Him first, I wanted to take my last breath.

I was convicted to the bone, and I was shaken to my very core. I didn't want to go on any longer. I felt my life was a complete waste and that I had totally messed everything up. I had waited so long to get married and now this happened! I was at my end until God opened my eyes to His undying love for me.

Even though I had been unfaithful to God by allowing the husband that I chose to control every aspect of me, God never left me. He stayed the course and for that I will always love Him. When my eyes were finally open to the error of my ways I repented and told God that I would never marry again unless He sent me someone that loved Him more. I ended up divorcing the husband of my choice and I learned a valuable lesson. We must trust God completely with our lives and what He has planned for us to fulfill our purpose in life.

~~~

Have you ever wanted something so badly that you lost focus when everything around you seemed to lose its luster, compared to what you desired appearing in clear view? That, my dear, is not balance. It is not the will of God for you to lose sight of who you are and disappear into the identity or shadow of someone else.

He does not desire for you to put your entire life, your dreams, or your plans on the back burner as if they have no value. Why should what God has purposed for you to do, be placed on a shelf to do nothing but collect dust? What has been placed in you is a treasure trove of hope and encouragement that someone else needs. *"It is time for you to realize that you are of great value, and the world will not be the same without you."* It is high time for you to *Come Out of the Shadows and Into the Light.*

We've all made mistakes. Shake yourself and get back up again. Brush yourself off and keep moving forward. Don't allow the mistakes of your past to define who you are. There is only one person who can define you, and His name is Jesus. You are fearfully and wonderfully made in the image of God, and there is no devil that can stop what God has planned for your life.

You are a "Woman of Purpose, Power, and Passion," with a destiny without limit! Not even the sky can place a border around what you are created to be and to do. Yes, we all have a past and possibly even up until a moment ago, we might have something that we are not proud of.

But guess what -- if we were perfect, we would not need God. We certainly would not need one another. So, what is that thing that has been drawing you like a magnet to its core? What is it that causes you to rise from your sleep and dream while you're awake? You know that thing that you just can't shake. What is the thing that you sometimes find yourself daydreaming about in the middle of the day when you're supposed to be doing something else? Sometimes you find yourself lost in thought, just for a moment; basking in the what ifs of life.

Well, that thing…that feeling will never go away. It will find you at every point of life. It will keep coming back until you recognize that thing is your purpose. Your purpose has a personality, and it will seek after you until it finally takes hold of the real you on the inside. It will cause you to stop hiding and propel you into the light, like a beam that cannot be hidden. Ultimately, you will have no choice but to be the person that you are called to be. Your purpose will begin to breathe louder, harder, and stronger, and it will demand your full attention. If you ignore this inner drawing to be who you are at your center, you will be miserable. Take it from me; hiding in the shadows of others is a temporal state of self-rejection that is highly overrated!

It's better to be the best you that you can be, and not be concerned about disappearing into the fabric of someone else just to be hidden in the seams of their personality.

God has a plan for you that is nicely wrapped up in the purpose of You! You, my dear, are a gift. So, wipe the tears from your eyes from what could have been, what should have been, or what will never be, and see yourself as a treasure from God to the earth. He has placed inside of you everything that you need to do what He has chosen you to do. Every ounce of His power resides in you as a child of God.

You can tap into His power twenty-four hours a day, and manifest what He put inside of you before you were even born. Yes, that's right! Everything that you need is already in you. You just need to seek the face of God for direction and trust Him to lead you every step of the way.

Some people may say, well I don't need God, or it doesn't take all that based on their level of intelligence, or analytical persuasion. But without God they would not even exist. So yes, to know one's purpose and to tap into the power of God to fulfill one's intended passion; it does take all that and more! There is no way that we could reach the essence of who we are created to be without having an intimate relationship with our heavenly Father.

Why do I make this statement? Well, all people are created in the image and likeness of God. So, we will by nature continually desire to be who He intended for us to be from the beginning.

15

If we try to be someone other than who we are, we will eventually come to the realization that our attempts will only yield fruitless results. Why? Because it's in us to be like Him! Running from who we are will only draw us right back to the source of our creation.

So again, I ask you, what is it that keeps you up at night? What is it that keeps drawing you back to the core of who you really are? Repeat after me. It's my purpose, full of power and passion. Now, say it again. It's my purpose, full of power and passion. Now, doesn't that feel better that you've finally said it out loud? Know that it's okay to be you! You don't have to hide any longer. Nobody else has the characteristics or even the same fingerprints as you.

So, embrace the dreams that God keeps giving you to fulfill. Do not allow one dream to drop to the floor and turn into dust to be simply swept into a dustpan and thrown into the trash. No dream is too small or too great for God to bring into full manifestation in your life.

There is nothing too hard for God. All you must do is believe and act upon the seeds of faith that are planted in your heart. He will do the rest.

However, that doesn't mean that everything will be easy, and that there will not be challenges along the way. It simply means that God will lead and guide you throughout the entire process if you depend on Him. You will never have to worry about Him leaving you to figure things out for yourself; what He begins, He finishes with excellence. It is His nature to do all things well.

We must trust Him to complete the work in and through us. Our past has no bearing on what we've been chosen to do. God knew all our challenges before we were born. He knew that we would choose others over Him. He knew that we would become so dependent upon people and things that our focus would get off balance. He knew that we would even reject Him. But He still chose us, and He still loves us.

That's right, He still loves me, and He still loves you! So, what can we do in response to His love for us?

We can express our love for Him by being who He has chosen us to be. You may be thinking right now that you don't really know who you are, or what you are chosen to do. That's okay; just seek His direction, and He will reveal who you are to you. And if you do know your purpose, then that's an even better reason to continually build an even more intimate relationship with Him, so He will always be glorified in your life.

Nevertheless, I will not take it for granted that everyone reading this book has received the Lord Jesus Christ into their heart as their personal Lord and Savior, so let's make sure of that right now. The word of God says in Romans 10:9,

"That if you confess with your mouth the Lord Jesus Christ, and believe in your heart that God raised Jesus from the dead, that you can be saved."

So right now, say these simple words to inherit the eternal abundant life in Christ. "Lord Jesus, forgive me of all my sins, wash me in Your blood, and cleanse me from all unrighteousness. I believe that You died on the cross and was buried, and on the third day God the Father raised You from the dead. And right now, Lord Jesus, I open the door to my heart, and I receive You into my heart as my personal Lord and Savior."

Now, that we have that taken care of that, what's next? The very next thing for you to do is to look around you. What do you see? How do you feel? What gets to you? What lights your fire to the point that you want to make a change? What brings tears to your eyes? These are all signs of who you are, and what you are called and chosen to do.

Start journaling on a daily basis and write down what you're passionate about. Your passion is tied to your purpose, and it will be evident by what pricks your heart.

Always keep your journal with you because you never know when you'll be inspired. And whatever you do, don't allow the enemy to trick you by saying that you don't know who you are, when you are staring yourself in the face every day! There is no need for confusion or lack of focus. All you must do is continually spend time with God and He will gently show you who you are over a period of time. He is a gentleman. He's never overbearing or forceful. He will give you time to adjust to who you really are.

In closing, make sure that you continually remind yourself daily that the Author and Creator of love, loved you first, and you are more than worth His investment.

You are a *"Woman of Purpose, Power, and Passion,"* called for such a time as this. To show forth His glory through the very essence of who He created you to be. When you feel yourself becoming overwhelmed by the magnitude of you, remember to depend upon God and He will give you the strength to do and to be who you already are!

CHAPTER REFLECTION:

1. What one thing from this chapter will you apply to your life?

2. Who can you trust to help you in areas of weakness?

3. What can you do daily to love yourself, and others?

Write down your responses to the above reflection in the *Woman of Purpose, Power and Passion Companion Journal*; and share what you have written with a confidant; who will help you to fulfill your God-ordained purpose.

Rein Johnson

Heireina Patrei Johnson, also affectionately known as "Rein" or "Lady Rein" in art, ministry, and authorship was born and raised in San Francisco, CA to Elder Huey P. Johnson and Evangelist Yuvetta Pryor. Her father, prior to his passing right before her birth, prophesied over her in the womb, indicating that she would become a dynamic woman of God carrying on his legacy of high-profile ministry and profound commitment to the cause of Christ, and that she would be chosen to bring healing and deliverance to nations. Rein was saved, anointed, and called to preach at the tender age of seven—a ministry prodigy often astounding those who experienced her keen insight, revelations, and theological/exegetical handling of the word.

Her ministry was largely developed in the Church of God in Christ where she held many positions in ministry until she was called to further advancement and was licensed as an Evangelist in the AME church prior to a call to support a non-denomination ministry geared toward the marginalized and oppressed. There is a story behind the ministry that is an unfortunate legacy of being prostituted at the age of four, being molested, being raped, dealing with abortion, domestic violence, low self-esteem, bulimia, and a host of other challenges that she ministered through. However, in 2011, Rein experienced an encounter with God that not only completely healed her, but also catapulted her into a ministry of healing and deliverance that would reach and change so many others. Currently, Rein is a highly sought-after Evangelist, Prophetess, Revivalist, Speaker, Life Coach, Inspirational Artist, and Author wherein she continues in the work of spreading what God has entitled "The Gospel of Transformation." Humbly, she works the ministry with a passion to see others healed and living in their purpose.

Speaking Engagement & Special Event Contact Information:

Heireina P. Johnson
Evangelist "Rein"
4151 Boo Lane
Stockton, CA 95206
PH: 209-912-9932
Email: hereinz@me.com

Chapter Two

A Plan for the Pain

---

*"Transformative purpose is birthed
from every struggle."*
—Rein Johnson

An excerpt from my book I Am Not Garbage:

I was nine (almost ten) years old when I became the walking dead, when he committed my murder. It wasn't the physical murder that claimed my soul and body, it was an emotional death that I was not prepared to encounter. Much too old to sit on his lap, it was somewhat odd that he beckoned me to do so. I had become so accustomed to his distant stares and questionable eyes that his sudden concocted "sweetness" startled me. I wasn't afraid of him on that day, but I was unsure and suspicious.

I walked over to him silently with my tongue pressed against the roof of my mouth and my hands sheepishly toying with the fabric inside my pants pockets. The way he grabbed my arm and drew me to him was lifeless and empty of the warmth I had once known. He wasn't mean or unloving, but he was eerily condescending, and for the first time as I stood

23

that close to him with his breath blowing hot against my cheek, I felt unsafe.

"Sit on my lap," he said in a tone I hadn't known before. The lump in my chest found its way to my throat and I was sure that any second, I would hurl. Looking back on it, I wish I had. I remember him asking me if I knew how much he loved me. I gave a soft and insecure, "Yes" before I buried myself again in my silence.

"Sit on my lap," he said again as he widened his long legs and lifted me onto them. It was an eerie sort of feeling as I felt him situating me so that I would be sitting exactly where he wanted. I felt his hand brush my leg and my insides began to flutter with that same sickness I'd known before in my life. I knew his touch, but this wasn't the same kind of caring touch that I had come to know in years past. I knew this touch and it immediately hurled me through time and space to the "Big Red Bed" I had known when my grandmother prostituted me away as a toddler. The brushing of my legs was about gratification that I didn't want to be subjected to. I felt the part of a father's body a daughter should never feel rise underneath me, and I scooted and shifted to avoid the feeling, to no avail. He simply shifted me back in position, and I was paralyzed with fear.

He rocked underneath me giving himself a personal massage with my body and let his hands press up and down my back.

*"I don't like this," I thought. I wanted to speak, but I couldn't find the words. I was shattered inside. I couldn't believe that he was doing this to me, **me**, his little girl. I didn't want his nasty hands on my back or his hot breath on the nape of my neck. Then suddenly, as if God had heard me and had given me a way of escape, an idea popped into my head and I quickly said, "I have to go to the bathroom." He seemed annoyed, but he let me go. I decided I'd stay in that bathroom until I heard him retreat to his upstairs bedroom, but I couldn't be sure of the next day or any other day after that. I needed a plan.*

I laid on my bed that night shocked and angry at what he had done with me. I couldn't sleep or think. I didn't feel safe enough to do either one. I thought about the conversation that I could have with my mother, but the bitter ending was always the same. My grandmother's words about me being a burden to my mother rang loudly in my ears and I knew I couldn't tell. Things weren't great in our house, but I just couldn't bear the burden of being responsible for the end of their marriage. I had a new little brother to consider, and my mother was pregnant with her second child by him. I did the only thing I knew to do back then, I cried.

Most nights had become the same. My mother retreated to her bedroom and my stepfather fumbled around in the kitchen and living room just outside my door. The nights had become so familiar to me that I often lay in the bed paralyzed. I tried with all my might to dart into a world away from the sickening activity each night, but there was never any relaxing or relief as long as this monster-like person existed on the other side of my door. I insulated myself and prepared for the rain each time by telling myself it would all be over soon, but it was never over. I always felt like I was being abused whether I was fully dressed or stark naked. I had become so ashamed of my body and myself.

Each occurrence was the same. The creaking of the door assured me of his presence. He closed it carefully and slowly while I lay usually on my side watching the light that he entered the room with slowly draw itself up from the floor and disappear. He would climb into my small bed and arch himself behind me. His hands would rub my back and other parts of my body. On occasion he would force me to touch him, but most of the time he chose to violate me as much as possible. I often wanted to scream, and I'd hoped my mother would walk in and catch him, but he was always slick and quick.

The first time I felt something awaken in me, it scared me. I hated myself because I thought it was a sure sign that I was secretly enjoying his repeated offenses. I sank deeper and deeper into depression and often thought about jumping out of our apartment window. I hated him for touching me, and I hated myself for having any feeling. I didn't understand the natural response to stimulus. All I knew was that this touching was bad, and if I had any pleasure in it, so was I. I didn't like it, but my body seemed to say different, and I was sorely confused. I told myself, "It's no wonder that God hasn't answered my prayers for the abuse to stop." I'm a nasty child who found a sense of pleasure in the unthinkable even if it was just once. I'm the "whore" my grandmother said I was. I'm the garbage she predicted. I deserve this abuse.

I didn't have anyone to talk to. I only knew the guilt and my secret shame. I believed that I had betrayed my mother when in fact it was my father that had betrayed me and my mother. I had become accustomed and all too familiar with consistent pain and it angered me. Everything in me wanted to snap.

As I recall those horrific nights as a scared and confused adolescent, I wish that I could tell you that my pain had originated with a few casual nights of sexual misconduct and inappropriate touching, for if I could, it would erase the truth of the abuse that started long before then—in my lineage to be exact. I wish the women in my family had not been so abused and hurt themselves that it traveled down my bloodline and caused my grandmother to trade a few hours of me as a four-year-old girl to a whore house for laughs and alcohol. If this were the beginning of the story; *my story*, then there would be no recollections of familial drunken stupors, all day whippings by my grandmother followed by hours and hours of speeches about how horrible I was, how much of a burden I was, and how evil and ugly I was destined to be. If there had been only the few instances I described above, then my stepfather's infidelity with my peer's mother, his visitation to crack houses, my mother's depression, and my ultimately feeling abandoned by everyone might not exist. But the story *didn't* begin or end there.

They say that we are our stories, and the truth is, I know this all too well. It amazes me that we can completely understand that what is happening to us is wrong and that the negative and hateful words being spoken over us are lies, yet those words and experiences have a way of penetrating the psyche so deeply and infiltrating the core of our souls— intensely and intricately weaving themselves into our beliefs and values, that we are doomed to repeat the pain of the past. Most times unknowingly, we cry out to it subconsciously, calling it forth like a mother to a child.

I hated being abused. In fact, for a long time, I let the hatred I felt for all of my abusers consume me. My grandmother was emotionally and spiritually sick, and she was an alcoholic. She was just plain torturous and evil. She got her kicks by doing and saying the most hateful things she could think of to say and do to me. My stepfather, his friends, and the many others who molested me were also sick, they were substance abusers, and they didn't *see* me. They didn't see the helpless little girl who was deathly afraid of them and their advances; they only saw me through pedophiliac eyes. I was a target to them. I wasn't freed from any of it until my mother divorced and moved away from them all, but even then, I had become bound to the prison of my subconscious mind.

Determined to protect myself, I developed an even more twisted sense of how to do so. I vowed that no one would ever take anything from me; instead, I willingly gave. I gave of my body, my heart, and even my money at a young age without knowing that I was trying to correct what had been done to me, and thereby I was creating more pain and more abuse. Even being raped in high school at fourteen and having the abortion thereafter did not motivate me to change. It scarred me for life, and the suicidal thoughts and semi-attempts were sure to follow; but nothing changed me. As intense as even the gospel was in my church, it wasn't reaching *me*. It wasn't reaching the pained core of me. In fact I was saved and called to ministry at the tender age of seven, I understood the spiritual atmospheres, the laying on of hands, the speaking of other tongues, prophetic encounters, and all of the emotional frenzies we called "spiritual," but I felt a lot like God had abandoned me because no one, not even those with the keenest spiritual insight or prophetic gifts could see me beyond my gifts and my anointing. At least, it wasn't made known to me.

I was a fiery little preacher with amazing insight on the Word, often astounding those around me, and I loved God with an intense love I can never explain, but deep down, I was trying to prove to God that I was worthy of His love and support. I wanted His help desperately. It was extraordinarily hard for me to accept the leaders of my church telling me how special and anointed I was and how great my ministry was destined to be when I was facing such turmoil at home and being tormented by memories. I needed proof. If God loved me so much, I needed Him to show me. So, simultaneously, I found myself competing not only for the attention of those around me, who I wanted desperately to love me, but for God's attention too.

I didn't want to be a target anymore. I didn't want to be confused anymore. I wanted respect. I wanted loyalty. I wanted to love. I just didn't know how to obtain it, and I would spend years, well into my adulthood, trying to bring closure to the pain of my past. I was growing in the ministry, pretending to be strong, and preaching around, over, and on top of all of my collected "stuff." I was an emotional hoarder. By day I was well put together—a diva on the outside while dying inside, but I could preach, I could sing, and I could even get others "delivered." Yet by night, I was still that scared little girl sleeping beneath the rubble of every memory; swallowed up in agony, but too proud to ask for help because "*ministers and leaders are supposed to be strong and any sign of weakness will render you ineffective.*"

So, I had to keep it together, and I had the routine down. I was taught that no matter what you have been through, God allowed it and ordained it for you to be used. I couldn't reconcile that teaching with all that I had been through for the sake of simply having a testimony that proves how good God is, so I remained silent. I even held a little anger towards the church because of it.

When God has a plan for you, it doesn't matter what you have been through. Your wrong thinking can't override it. Sometimes it gets just ugly enough for you to turn your attention to Him, to learn something, and to be pulled out of the gaping holes in your reality and out of the grasp of despair.

In 2010 I met a person that I thought was a wonderful man. Still on the path of "finding love," that I thought would in turn heal me at my core, and still preaching over and on top of all of it presuming I was "OK." I didn't see the signs, or I ignored them. I missed the alarms. I even traded in my core values for sex and planned a wedding way too fast. I didn't see the ghosts he was running from or the cloud of impending doom that followed him into my home and into my bedroom. I was frolicking in the imaginary daises and the sunshine because "resolution" was finally here. So, I quickly made him the center of my world—my ultimate focus. Despite my Christian upbringing I moved him into my home, and when he immediately started talking marriage, I was thrilled. I was working fifty plus hours per week and taking on a full-time school load, so he was there spending more time with the kids, cooking, and cleaning and managing the house, and it felt like everything was coming together. I had help. I had support, and let's be real, I had a man around the house, and we know as women how good that makes us feel. So, rather than seeing what I *needed* to see, which was all my areas of compromise and the places where my wisdom was not in activation, I frolicked in the daisies. I even ignored previous warnings from friends who knew of his history. I chose to believe him, and because he lived with me, I concluded that I would see for myself. I was right about "seeing for myself."

One night I had a prophetic dream, not knowing at the time it was prophetic. I found myself, my former fiancée, and my three sons smack dab in the middle of a tsunami. I was the one desperately trying to save my oldest son and bring my family to safety. We were running from this storm with everything we had. I woke up and I mentioned it to him, and you would have thought he had seen a ghost. Finally, something in my spirit connected to heaven, and I knew he knew something that I did not. I unsuccessfully tried to dismiss the dream and the feeling.

Soon after, the blinders started coming off. The disappearing acts started. Where we had never been afraid to leave our cell phones around, he was suddenly more guarded and secretly texting and deleting messages. He started losing pounds very rapidly. Everything was becoming so much more suspicious. He had a creative lie for everything, but being the analytical researcher I am, I began my search for information. While I made myself physically sick going through timesheets, receipts, texts, emails, and drawers, the answers had been in front of me all along. To make a long story short, I discovered infidelity, and lies about his job supposedly opening a new location in another city and his having to stay out there and work. I discovered that he was trying to rent an apartment because he believed he was going to get away with having a place to have orgies and homosexual relationships on the side. I discovered that the drug use I had been warned about was real, which explained the weight loss he was lying about. He had his entire routine carefully planned, and I had fallen for it hook, line, and sinker.

As I packed his things, I remember collapsing over and over under the weight of hurt, panic attacks, and depression until finally I retreated to the bathroom. I sat on the floor and sent out the mass text letting everyone know the wedding was off, and humiliated and ashamed I sat there with tears just streaming down. There was no going back. I ran the bathwater to see if a relaxing soak would help, but I was so weighted I hadn't noticed the water and the bubbles spilling over to the floor and surrounding me. I was in a trance—a devastated place, and the water surrounding me was like an outward representation of what was happening on the inside.

I remember saying repeatedly, "God, help me." There was really nothing else to say. Every pain I could imagine came rushing up to the surface and I was numb when my entire body wasn't aching. I couldn't form a thought or complete a sentence beyond, "God, help me." As I reached up to lean over the tub and shut off the water, I heard the softest of voices say to me, "Trust Me."

Trusting God didn't prove to be an easy feat. In a matter of weeks, I lost my job, my house, and my car. My oldest two children decided they wanted to go live with their father, and my mother came home and said she had cancer. It was test after test and trial after trial, and I was absolutely devastated. I spent six months held up in the tiny loft above my mother's house crying out to God, shedding weight, forgiving, healing, trusting, and believing that God had a plan even through all the hell. I wrote the book *I Am Not Garbage* that God instructed me to write, and while it was not easy to do, so much came to the light. It was a season of me and God walking through the corridors of my being and uncovering every demonic lie and spirit that had set itself up to destroy me. Even the religious anecdotes prescribed to me by the leaders in the church trying to explain away my suffering were expelled. It is where God gave me transformational insight that would change my life, and the lives of so many others. It was where I was officially moved from being called to being chosen.

Why is all of this relevant to you, my friend? You may be like me; I grew up in church all of my life, and I spent so much time trying to figure out what my "church" ministry was that I had not considered what my **planetary purpose** was. I was anointed to preach, to teach, to sing, to praise dance, to administer and lead, and I was on every committee I could be on. I was over the youth and the children, involved in evangelism, Sunday school, and Bible Study, and I was in most choirs… purposeless. It isn't that those things were not assets to the ministry. In fact, doing those things strengthened my knowledge and my faith in God. They enhanced me as a person and as a minister of the gospel, and for that I am extraordinarily grateful, but I was neglecting the inner hero that we all have within us. I was honoring the called part of my life, but not the chosen part.

Some people are chosen to be church frontline soldiers and carry on the work of the ministry predominantly, but believe me when I tell you that there is always more to the story of what we are chosen to accomplish in our time on the planet. All of us are called to be an answer to something, but so few make it to the chosen stage because we are so conditioned to allow life to just happen to us, instead of working to find and become the legacies we were meant to be.

Romans 12:2 says, "*Do not be conformed to this world, but be transformed by the renewal of your mind that by testing*

35

you may discern what is the will of God, what is good, what is acceptable, and perfect." (ESV)

When God gave this to me, I thought I understood it. Like most Christians, I thought the text was about staying away from sin and not doing anything that mirrored the "world's" standard. I believed that by being free of anything that did not reflect God appropriately, I was renewed in my mind, so to speak, and I was obedient to the Word. It wasn't that my attempts to remain sinless were unnoticed, but God asked me how much of the world did I really know. I discovered that I only knew the world that I had lived in. I knew very little of this secular society that I maintained with all my heart to keep a good distance from to mirror Christ, and I knew extraordinarily more about this world of pain, verbal abuse, molestation, rape, abortion, and everything I else I had lived through. While the original text interpretation was not completely off, God wanted me to go deeper and then to teach others the same revelation.

Your world, my friend, is made up of everything that you have experienced. Even if you have not been through what I have, believe me when I tell you there is some dysfunction in all of us that needs truth and healing to be applied to it. God does not these experiences to define us. My truth is that I was absolutely shaped by them. I developed patterns of serial dating, illicit sex, wrong relationships, trust issues, and the list goes on. I believed things about myself, not even knowing I had those beliefs. God wants to take a walk with you down the corridors of your life. He wants to stop and help you have dismissal and return to sender conversations with demonic forces hanging out in your heart, soul, and mind. He cares more about your wrong thinking and your subconscious secrets that have the ability to destroy you than He does about your "religious (or non-religious) living." His ultimate desire is that we be made completely whole from the inside out– not just in lip service, but in life service.

John 4:24 says, *"God is Spirit, and His worshippers must worship Him in spirit and in truth."*

We have the stuff of the spirit. We know how to cry profusely. Many of us have a holy language we pray in. Even those who don't profess salvation know how to turn to God when in need and know how to express appreciation to God at random if they so choose. Worship is not a matter of how intense the gratitude, how profuse the tears, how sincere the praise, or how deep the holy language, worship is about the truth.

Most of us never really reach the threshold of worship because we won't acknowledge the truth of who we are and what we have faced in a way that heals us from it. In the Bible, priests fell out dead for less offense. They were simply unclean trying to come into the presence of God. We come before God with so much baggage and expect that it is God's job to sift through it when it is really our job to *bring it* to God by way of the truth. It is to our benefit to be healed, but we repetitively choose ignorance or suppression of the truth. We make attempts to leave the past in the past, but the past unchecked, uncorrected, or left to roam finds its way undoubtedly into our present and future. It is not easily dismissed by affirmations, religious ritual, or avoidance. It *must* be healed.

There's another text, Romans 8:28, and I love the New Living translation because it explains it more thoroughly: And we know that God *causes* everything to work together for the good of those who love God and are called according to his purpose for them. As I noted earlier, there is a theology that suggests that what we go through is somehow prescribed by God to work out a testimony and to prove the glory of God. The suggestion that God would allow a helpless little girl to be prostituted, molested, and raped did not exactly draw me closer to God.

What I came to understand in the healing process is that it is not that God intended for me to go through all of that for a testimony or a ministry to be birthed, but He understood clearly what family I would be born into, what choices would be made, what the struggles would be, and what I would have to face. God created answers before the problems existed, and He determined that you and I would be those answers. You and I would be resurrected from the death dealing pasts we have known, healed, and chosen to work for God's good.

My friend, I want you to understand that there is and has always been a plan for your pain. There has always been a divine purpose that would not only pull you out of the slum of yesterday, but a plan that would involve you being chosen to reconcile so many others to their complete healing. Our planetary purpose is to be healed and to heal; to be the incarnate "good" that this text speaks about.

Because God's view is Kingdom and purpose driven to what affects nations, your planetary purpose is to heal, and to take those experiences and revelations to the world in whatever way God leads. Your healing becomes your gospel (the truth) that needs to be shared with the world. That is what being a woman of purpose, power and passion is all about! What is your planetary purpose? What have you suffered? Where are your deepest hurts? What are the thoughts you suppress? What are the patterns that need to be broken off your life? What are the memories you dread reliving? What are those things you'd rather forget? You are the end of your own and someone else's struggle. Again, there is and has always been a plan for your pain. God just wants you to sit with Him long enough to find out what He wants you to do with it. Will you accept that challenge?

As I close, I want to prophetically speak to your spirit and command the hero in you to come forth! I speak to every dry place, every broken place, and every emotional lie causing bankruptcy in your heart, mind, body, and soul to be devoured by the power of the Holy Spirit. I declare complete healing from the inside out is yours for the asking. Every foul spirit and its residue must be bound up and cast out in the matchless name of Jesus Christ *today*!

I call forth your greatness, your wisdom, your hope, your tenacity, your peace, your resolve, and your power to break chains, destroy yokes, break down barriers, demolish walls, cast out spirits, and tear down demonic kingdoms.

You are not your yesterday. You are greater than your mind can ever reconcile. Arise woman of purpose, power, and passion; your destiny is calling as hurt is calling to be healed. I release you from the prison of the past into the promise of peace.

Philippians 2:5-8, *"You must have the same attitude that Christ Jesus had, though He was God, He did not think of equality with God as something to cling to. Instead, He gave up His divine privileges; He took the humble position of a slave and was born as a human being. When He appeared in human form, He humbled Himself in obedience to God and died a criminal's death on a cross."*

I don't know what your cross is, beloved, but I speak right now to every place of fear, every place of doubt, every seed of distraction, and to every place of delay and declare that the Kingdom of God *is* coming, and the Will of God **will** be done in your life. I release you from the fear of what must be addressed, what must be lost, what must be given up, and what must be faced, and replace it with peace, comfort, and confidence in God, knowing that whatever He wills is for the greater good.

May the intense favor of God rest and rule in your life, and every promise and purpose be made complete through your agreement with who God says you are! There is great need of you woman of God. Just as God has given me "The Gospel of Transformation" for you, I am in need of the gospel He has given you for me. Arise!

CHAPTER REFLECTION:

1. What is your purpose after the pain? Every being has a purpose on the planet; a legacy they must leave; something they are divinely called to cure. That purpose can be found as we review our past experiences—the deeply rooted stuff we wish to suppress, the pain we wish to forget, the thoughts and memories we wrestle with, are all clues to what we have the potential to become the answer to. Where do you hurt the most? That is what you will have the most power and spiritual authority to heal.

2. What are the unhealthy patterns and processes that have attached themselves to you as they relate to who you believe you are, what you believe you deserve, what holds you back in life, and what shapes your relationships with others and the world at large around you?

3. What commitment will you make to yourself today to be healed, to be healthy, to be free, and then to give? When you find that internal healing, what will you deposit back into the universe? How will you help others? What can you identify as your "Purposed Plan?"

Write down your responses to the reflections above in the *Woman of Purpose, Power and Passion Companion Journal*, so that you can apply the principles of this chapter.

Berta Jean

This Empowerment Diva received her degree in cosmetology, passing the CA State Board, receiving her License in 1993. Berta Jean has been depositing empowering words of wisdom into the lives of women through beauty and counsel for the last 20 years. Finding herself not only sewing in hair, but weaving and bonding lives, she found herself becoming less of a stylist and more than a life coach. Berta Jean returned to school to further her education in an area she desired the most, Human Social Services with a minor in Corrections.

Working as a conflict mediation counselor with O.U.S.D., Berta Jean took to the streets, jails, shelters, and churches to encourage and inspire young women from her similar background by promoting higher learning, home economics, healthy living, and spirituality and life care. In 2006, Berta Jean launched Boss Lady Productions, an event planning service that produces and hosts events for large low-income families, teen parents, and victims of violent crimes. Through consistent mentorship opportunities as a hair stylist, Berta Jean wrote her first women's motivational book titled *A Divas Daily Devotional* in 2010, pleading with women to spend more time pampering themselves to become just as pretty and attractive on the inside as they appear on the outside. Accrediting all of her accomplishments to her faith, Berta Jean gives all praises to God, for it is He who has done great things!

She has only been a witness! Her charismatic poetry and popular interviews have been featured on *Talk Girl Talk Radio*, *The Nikki Rich Show*, *LA Firm Fashion Magazine, Eureka Revealed Christian Magazine*. Her Poetry earned her Heritage Poet of The Year.

Speaking Engagement & Special Event Contact Information:

Berta Jean
P.O. Box 99586
Emeryville, CA 94662
PH: 510-812-2116
Email: bossladiproductions@gmail.com

CHAPTER THREE

Climbing Hills in Heels

"It's not what we stand in, but what we stand on that makes the difference."
—Berta Jean

I'm the first born of my mother's six children. She gave birth to me at age fourteen. My mother died when she was forty-six. My life has been like a scary movie. I keep covering my eyes, but it doesn't stop me from being chased. I have seen several people lying dead on the ground after I survived ducking bullets right alongside of them. I've had several physical fights with individuals, and I've also been jumped. I've been robbed at gunpoint, sold drugs, had gold teeth, and been a rapper. Some have called me a "diva" as they see my chosen attire, the blonde hair, the make up the high heels, and let's not forget, the attitude. Others have said that I'm just too "hood." Fact is I'm both. I'm a "hood diva" that emerged from one of the roughest neighborhoods in Oakland, California. These experiences make me equipped, tried, tested and true, and this is my story!

When I was about 8 years old, my grandmother wanted full custody of me because my mom chose to move away from our hometown in Berkeley, California to crime infested West

Oakland, California. One day while outside playing in my front driveway I heard "Run, Berta, run!" It's what my mother instructed me to do, so I ran.

I looked back to see what I was to run from, and it was my grandmother. I couldn't understand for my tiny life why I was running from the very person I had been running to for days, weeks, and even months on end. I lived with her in the same house from the day I was born. I've slept in her arms, laid in her lap, drank from her coffee mug, and went to the store with her empty coke bottles in exchange for a dime to buy penny candy. This is my favorite person in the world and my mother told me to run from her! I stopped dead in my tracks mid-way up the driveway; I looked both ways to see whom I was closest to when my right arm was almost yanked out of its socket. My mother won the chase; she grabbed me first and yelled to my grandmother's face, "You ain't gettin' my baby!" It was that day that I heard my mother loud and clear. This message was not to be muffled by my aunts, uncles, or even her own mother telling me 'yes' when she said 'no.' I watched my grandmother return to her car without saying a word to me. There were no smiles between us, no hugs, and no good-byes; there was no connection at all.

My eyes began to water, but my mother stopped my tears before they could completely form. She looked at me hard as she pulled my arm and said, "You better not cry." This pain was so big to swallow that it must have broken something inside of me in order for it to stay inside. This is where I learned to turn off my emotions, and to just start running away.

My mother preached that she would never raise another duplicate of "her" in her home. She had an expectation of the girls she was raising, and it started with me, the first-born. She hid her entire pregnancy until my delivery at 11:39am on Nov 29th, 1971, whose father's name reads "Withheld" on the birth certificate. I was conceived in secret, born into drama, and then raised in confusion. I was running from herself for feeling like a mistake and running from her family for fear of resembling a scar of infidelity.

My dad was also fourteen when I was born, and he was very much unprepared to be a father. He was around until I was in kindergarten. A new relationship is what I believed kept him away from me. I saw him with his then wife and their other family once when I was eleven, and his broken promise to attend my baseball game upset me to the start of running track. I ran from him so many times on that field I thought I had completely ran him out of my system. That only lasted for a year. The following year, when I was twelve, my mother told me I was conceived during an outdoor concert with my father who was dating her sister at the time. She said she only wanted "one thing" from him and she ended up with two. My mother summed up my father as being "soft." She

said he was "something good to look at, and that's about it."
My mother told me my father was a smart man, college
educated turned pimp, and then he changed and got into
church heavily.

At that moment she was combing my hair she said, "But
today your daddy don't want a daughter, he want some dope,
so stop asking me about him." It all began to fit–the tensions,
the attitudes, and the fights–it all kept me running, and
running, and running. At age fourteen, watching my
mother's own demise to crack cocaine, I started running the
streets. By age sixteen, I had run past the idea of a father's
love and jumped right into my first love and my first STD. I
had a sexually transmitted disease before I had a period. I
was hospitalized for having contracted one of the worst
undetected strains of chlamydia. During my hospital stay, I
had a visitor bring me flowers. The flowers were from the
man that had given me this infection, but he was not
delivering them. I noticed the visitor came with two identical
floral arrangements. The visitor informed me that this man
who had given me this infection was sending the same
flowers to the same floor of the same hospital because the
mother of his children was only a few doors away from me
with the same infection. This man was much older than I
was; I had such an expectation of what this man was to be. I
expected him to be more than my father and everything my
mother said he wasn't! I ran from that hospital, and I ran

from that relationship right into another relationship with those same expectations.

My new relationship lasted for a little over eight years. It would be nice to say that something finally worked out, but I can't. What I can say is how I ran from house to house and slept on floor after floor with this man. I ran from corner to corner in the bedrooms he would beat me in. I ran from doctor to doctor with the wounds and pains. I ran my mouth to my family about everything else except what was being done to me.

I was at restaurant recently when a man approached me and my best friend of over 30 years. He said, "It's good to see that you guys are still friends." We all smiled and continued the conversation, wanting to know how and where we'd previously met. When the stranger shared that he had remember us both from mutual friend's birthday party where I was yanked from the dance floor by my then boyfriend. He grabbed my hair and dragged me to the car some two blocks away. The stranger closed the conversation by saying, "I wished you were my sister that night." As the stranger brought his story to a close, he wished us well and went on his way as I stood there recalling the rest of that special night.

I was thrown in a car and slapped in my face repeatedly by my "soulmate" as he drove to my new apartment. Once the car stopped, I jumped out quickly and brandished a big knife, a baby sword of some kind. I had it hidden on the passenger side of the car for the day I would need to kill or be killed. I had enough, I stood there and made my first and last threat to kill this man if he hit me again and I ran away. I ran like Tina ran from Ike the night of her last fight (*What's Love Got to Do with It,* 1993).

Some 20 years later I call him "friend," a title I thought would never get past my heart to reach my lips, but today I stand undefeated and unafraid of my former contender! I feel like Floyd Money Mayweather. My fights have made me a champion of many battles.

Today, I'm a true warrior because of him, and forgiveness has made me rich in spirit because I ran right into worship. I began rebuilding a relationship I had left at age sixteen. I recommitted myself to the Lord. It's only in this relationship that I was able to lose fear, keep my peace, experience real joy, and know real love.

I finally got married being only twenty-four years old and found that I could not conceive a baby naturally. I had developed so much scar tissue from that infection in my teens it was affecting my marriage. What was worse is I had to see this man who had destroyed my womb running around with his many children while my new husband and I ran back and forth to doctors. I took hormones and tests, as well as had sex on schedules. I even grew a beard because of the hormones, only to watch my baby run down the shower drain as it fell outside of my body. I just stood there so angry and broken as my husband held the remains until the paramedics arrived. I in turn ran from my husband, I ran from intimacy, I ran to birth control as I claimed to be running from a repeat of joy and faith stealing practices. I ran from my marriage to food. I told myself that it was not meant for me to be a mother, so I no longer wanted to be a wife.

I was twenty-six running from table to table and plate to plate until I was pound for pound topping out at 340lbs. I ran from being desired as I hid behind the Lord! Everything I was doing to my body, my self-esteem, and even my husband was all okay because of my claim, "the Lord is on my side." Not so! God was not pleased, and neither was I.

The Lord had given me a word to educate myself. I had always had a desire to be of good service to others when the Lord instructed me to start being of good service to me. I went back to school. As I began to transform my mind, my body followed. I parked my brand-new car and bought me a bicycle, I rode it everywhere I went. I got moving again in new circles of people, new foods; I got a new apartment and a new bed. I had a *Dr. Juanita Bynum* "no more sheets" moment.

I went to see *Dr. Bynum* at a conference along with my mother and grandmother. We had a minor accident on the way to the conference and it caused us to run extremely late. I was so mad at this point because I knew we had lost any chance of getting a floor seat. That evening from the nosebleed section of the balcony; *Dr. Bynum* called us down to the floor. The Lord told her there was a strong lineage in the balcony, three generations of strong women who almost didn't make it that night, "you had an accident because the enemy did not want you all to get this word." I was thinking back on how my mother wanted to go home after the wreck, but my grandmother and I knew better. I will never forget that moment. I changed. We all changed.

After running into a junior college to study human social services, I ran right into a biblical theology course for evangelists. I was so immersed in the bible and my education that I missed an entire decade of what the world was doing. I was completely out of touch with what people my age were into socially. Rap music was thriving, I had been a rapper and spoken word poet, but now I didn't even know who *Tupac Shakur* was. I didn't learn of him until after his death. That's how much I was running from the world, my friends, and especially my family. I was never in attendance for any of the gatherings that I had fought with my abusive boyfriend to attend.

I turned down all the important events like weddings, birthdays, baby showers, promotions, and milestone celebrations. These were events I would not only have attended, but I would have had a helping hand in putting it all together. But for some reason I rarely went anywhere other than church. Not that church was a bad thing; it was being used for my doing bad at that time. I was hiding behind religion and religious practices. I didn't know how to love beyond the church walls. If you didn't attend church, you couldn't attend my gatherings. If you didn't attend church, I didn't attend your gatherings. Don't stop by my house if you can't stop by the Lord's house. This is the way I loved. My love had so many conditions because I had been conditioned to place conditions on everything.

You sow you reap; you give you receive; you work you eat, you break you pay! Pain will make you do things to avoid "feeling" again, including using the "Word" to do so.

When you are "unhappy" being alone, you are hiding.

When you are "happy" being alone, you are focused.

Reuniting with myself, my family, and my friends gave me the foundation to stand still. I had been running past these people and places so hard and so often that I missed my season in some blessed places; therefore, I was missing my blessings repeatedly.

Well, not this time. I began walking into each season high stepping to stand still and looking good while doing so. I had to bridge my church family with my own family relatives and my friends. I later found that there was greater power in the numbers. We became one of the biggest and most supportive circles to be found. My friends are women of statue and confidence. Most of them are talented and business or goal driven. The women in my family are women of faith and have been in marriages for more than thirty years now. My uncles are old pimps turned family men. They had more to offer me than I realized when it came to the reality of relationships and expectations of men. I now stood as a somewhat sister to my aunts and uncles. Our conversations were so much more mature as I had grown out of a dictatorship with the O.G.'s *(Original Gangstas)*.

I was standing toe-to-toe, heel-to-heel in the height, depth, and width of conversation with those of great wisdom and experience. I was surrounded by blessings and living miracles and at one time I didn't even care about them at all.

I ran back into pieces of my old self, my sense of humor, my natural beauty, my hair, and my clothing. But something was still missing. I was just turning thirty and I was still wearing the small square Sunday-only edition of high-heeled shoes, my girlfriends where wearing stilettos that I hadn't even heard of. My same best friend took me out to get my first pair of stilettos; they were Steve Madden with a 6in chrome heel. I was so confident that I was wearing those shoes I bought two pair. We left the mall and headed to Pac-N-Save

Grocery Store. Once inside the store my girl branded the shoes from the bag and said, "Welcome to training day." She had me grab a shopping cart for support and walk the long slippery isle of the grocery store. Clinging to the shopping cart for dear life, my only task was to make it to the shelf, grab an item, and get back to the cart without dying. Ten steps, Berta, you can do it just grab the milk down and step, step, step. I did it; I did it over and over until the isle became my runway. I left the store high stepping in those heels and never looked back. My running shoes were now tied up in a shopping bag and locked in the trunk.

I began to walk so tall from that day forward. I walked tall in so many new boundaries. I walked tall in celibacy, higher learning, and goal setting. I now had a prettier foot to put down when it came to my standards. I became really focused on my character and how I presented myself and my home. If my girlfriend can't have a drink without getting drunk, then I don't have a drink with her. If your bathroom is nasty and your kitchen isn't clean, I wouldn't eat or sleep in your home. I may not even come inside anymore. If you're out in Costco buying bulks of ranch dressing, but never get or keep home necessities such as toilet paper, deodorant, bath soap, and laundry detergent, then you shouldn't be in a relationship. If your children are not well mannered and disciplined, I will not go out in public with you and your kids. I can't chase any bad kids in my heels. These are some of the things I practiced while standing alone focused.

Also, while standing alone in wait for whatever God had next, I developed the *before dark* rule. Everything I did, I did it before dark. To keep my celibacy, any male company (if ever I had any at home) had to be gone from my apartment way before dark. I met most of my company away from my apartment in public places. Meeting a man in several public places can confirm if he's free and single. If he continues to meet your terms you can *stand*. If you're able to meet his terms you can *stand*. If he doesn't have any terms, you should watch out or *walk* out. Remember not to *run* away because you will either pass somebody up or run into somebody! To keep my weight down I didn't eat anything after dark. I went into a low carb lifestyle of selectively choosing my sugar, bread, and potato intake, and not going overboard. Knowing my limits and triggers helped me to keep over 100lbs off for that last ten years. Late night after church eating and that "I'm not dating anyone," eating with your girlfriends is a big fat NO. I still go up and down in weight as we all do and being able to identify it and change it is the key. To keep my social life disciplined I went to all the barbeques, pool parties, brunches, celebrations, and sporting events, anything that ended before dark. I *stood* on all these practices until I remarried.

One beautiful day I was in heels walking tall into a corner store. I had stopped at the nearest one when I began to die of thirst. I was heading to the back of the store to the refrigerator when I saw this equally beautiful orange man standing there "sunshine" I'm thinking as he's staring me up and down.

The Lord knows I love an orange man, but I didn't blink, I kept my cool, I acted like I didn't notice him noticing me. I stood there in line until I grew uncomfortable by the presence of the orange man; I just walked toward the door. The store clerk called out to me, "Hey, you didn't pay!" I turned and pointed to the orange man and said, "He got it." I then turned and told the orange man, "You owe me something for looking so long." I walked out, I got in the car, and drove away from the store, only to run into the orange man a few moments to our destination. And the rest is history. The orange man became my friend. For the next three years we checked in on each other, before dark, without sex, and without being drunk and high. We dealt with our feelings and urges by communicating about the experiences of our prior relationships.

We married and remained friends. I was now able to hang out, party, travel, study, and pray with my husband. It's not been a perfect relationship, but it's how the relationship came about that was perfect for me. *I stood for something, and it fell for me!* That is how I explain my husband finding me. I stood in faith, I walked in confidence, and I have planned to climb many hills through different seasons of my life with him, if God agrees. Today just to see my husband, I stand in visitation lines, walk through metal detectors, and rest on concrete furniture. I walk into a prison real tall wearing my best heels with my brightest smile when I'm broken, disappointed and confused inside. This is what I'm currently standing in right now this minute, July 7th, 2013.

Many days I've screamed, "This is not what God called me to do." This cannot be the plan for my life! These are the things I would tell myself. I was angry that this was my husband, why not somebody else's? I was hurt by my husband's actions; his behavior made me feel so un-loved and completely embarrassed. I then became scared of losing my foundation with him and having to *stand* alone.

At one point I was so angry, so hurt, and so afraid that I dug deep and pulled out those old running shoes. I fell short and I ran around flat out wrong! I didn't stand as I had been able to. I ran away with the first twenty percent of a relationship full of what I believed that I had been missing. This relationship never amounted to much of anything. But during my run with the twenty percent, it appeared to be everything! It was only when I stopped running with it and looked at it standing still that I realized it never added up to the height of what I was to *stand* for! This was for "me" of all persons. I've been called, favored, prepared, blessed and sent forth to *stand*! But even I didn't believe that while I was running.

So when you're thinking about running please remember this: what you *stand* on determines what you can *stand* in. I fumbled and dropped my *faith* because I was *running* with it! Sometimes we are called to just **stand!**

Today, when it comes to my husband, I don't overthink it, and I don't over plan it. I love watching the Lord unfold it. I now tell myself, "Maybe I will walk with him or maybe I will walk alone; I will only stand because today I am equipped to do so."

Having my father reenter my world and be a part of my wedding was a great blessing. His walk back into my life and down that isle in that season greatly made up for his walk out of my life in my youth. There was a day when I claimed to have never needed a man, but on this day, this was the man I needed the most. In rhinestone-covered heels, I stood in forgiveness once again. I'm no longer seeking a father out of the men I'm attached to. Instead, I have an active, supportive confidant who approves and admires my marriage, even in its temporary demise.

My father has been a pillar of understanding in a time I was creating a typhoon of emotional problems for myself. I must admit that my father may not shine the brightest in my darkest moments, but to know that he's there when I need him has made him an asset instead of an old liability.

Looking back on some of our many good days, most of the time I walked around barefoot. My husband would say that I'm as country as four rows of planted okra. Maybe so but standing on the bare concrete represents more than what my husband may ever know. My mother did this all the time, and I inherited the sock destroying habit as well. The kids would be out in front in their socks jumping rope, or with me and my mom playing Jacks in ours. We were such big kids. Sometimes we would sit for hours on end eating, drinking, playing music, and talking with my grandmother whose front porch was just across the lawn.

Recently, while in our socks, my mother and I were sitting on her front porch as we often did. A woman that we didn't know grunted out to my mother, "Where are your shoes? You always out here with no shoes on." My mother's response to the woman was, "Don't worry about my shoes unless you can walk in them."

I did not respond out loud but was thinking of how expensive my heels were resting in plain view. I knew this woman didn't know to whom she was speaking. I wanted her to see what all we had to put on our feet. "My momma got Jordan's in here, lady!" That's what I wanted to say until my mother said out loud what I've kept in my heart until today.

My mother continued that conversation with me as the woman went on her way. My mom said, "Berta, don't mess

60

with people's feet. You can't judge a woman's shoes because you could be wearing them next. Never judge her walk or it will quickly become your next step." I've judged a person's trials and tribulation until their problems found my shoe size. That is how I quickly became very comfortable in my 'running shoes.' Not wanting to change myself, I consistently changed my surroundings, running from one crowd to the next. *Showing off my shoes…*

That experience made me think back to a time in my teens. My mother came to us and asked if we had been taking food from the freezer or eating all the leftovers before she got home from work. After we denied any wrongdoings, my mother set out on her own investigation. As we were leaving for our normal weekend trip to Berkeley to be with family and friends, my mother did something she had never done before. She pulled the car over immediately, as we turned the corner, she took a bat from the trunk put it up front and proceeded to drive around the block. As we approached our apartment at a high speed, my mother jumped from the car, bat in hand to nab one of the two girls climbing out of our kitchen window with armfuls of our food. With my running shoes on I was at my mother's aid to catch the girls that ran. We marched them to their apartment. Their mom stood in the doorway with no shoes on, with cracked and broken feet. She explained how she had been preparing the stolen food for her and her girls, as times were hard for them. I later understood why my mom had not accepted the repayment arrangement and why she agreed to give them the food. It was all in the feet. My mother saw that we could have easily been in those same shoes.

As I've grown, I've realized I cannot run as fast, as hard, and as long as I used to. The ground then seemed so level and flat. It was straightforward with my goals in plain view. Now with bad knees and mountains in front of me, I have no clue as to what is waiting on the other side. I'm now climbing. I'm stretching myself to new heights standing tall in my ability to achieve whatever awaits me on the other side. I didn't learn to walk in heels until I was thirty years old, so it is never too late. I love them. I feel all grown up. I feel like a lady, because they help me to keep it classy, to stand in peace when the "hood" me wants to surface. Doors are being prepared for each one of us in this lifetime. Some will be open, but many will be closed. *I must stand until I can walk through or walk out! I will not run again! No, I will not run again...*

I realize that there are battles coming in life that can be met in the shoes I stand in because I rest them on something as solid as my faith.

As women, we face most of our greatest challenges in high-heeled shoes. We stand in our discriminatory places of business, daily overcoming rejection. We stand in churches for hours on end enduring to receive of our beliefs. We stand in funerals teary eyed, and grief stricken. We stand in courtrooms facing divorces and custody battles. We attend schools, visit offices, and stand in lines, host meetings and much more reaching, stretching, and climbing each of those hills in heels, because we were designed to do so!

I want women standing in prison shower shoes and homeless women with their soles falling a part to know that they also can start again in those shoes. I want all my baby sisters out there in the hoods running from themselves, the abusive relationships, drugs, alcohol, the gunshots and violence that surround you, you women are my sisters, my best friends, my moms and aunties, I'm not running from you! I'm running to you, for you, and with you, until you too can climb your hills in heels.

CHAPTER REFLECTIONS:

1. What are you running from?
2. What are you standing on?
3. What are you prepared to climb?

Write down the answers to the reflections to the above questions in the *Woman of Purpose, Power and Passion Companion Journal*, so that you can step into a new dimension of your life in Christ by faith in action!

Janie Bess

Janie P. Bess is a writer, author, and activist. Her books, *Visions* and *Wife in the P.I.*, provide a revealing look inside her life as a U.S. Air Force wife and mother of five.

She raised her children, including her deaf-blind son, during difficult times when support for families with disabled children was limited. Janie's stories provide a revealing look inside her personal struggle to raise a family and overcome obstacles as she takes readers on a faith-inspired journey of the human spirit.

Janie lives in Northern California with her husband, David. She founded a nonprofit organization to lend support to other writers and leads the group through interactive workshops.

Speaking Engagement & Special Event Contact
Information:

Janie P. Bess

1652 Texas Street Ste. 247

Fairfield, CA. 94533

PH: 877- 629-7369

Email: JaniePbess@yahoo.com

Web: www.writersresourcecenter.net

CHAPTER FOUR

No Room at the End

"You are a direct reflection of your heavenly Father, and He has great plans for you." –Janie Bess

---

I was tired of making excuses explaining to the nurses on duty, "Oh, my husband and daughter called over an hour ago, saying they're on the way." I pretended to be calm, but I was worried after two hours had gone past. "I hope nothing's happened; they should've been here by now." I called home to tell my husband that I was released and waiting on a ride to the rehab facility in Fairfield.

"*Your* daughter has the car; she had to make an important run this morning. As soon as she returns, we should be on our way."

While waiting on them to pick me up, I opened my new hard back luggage case and did a quick inventory of my belongings carefully placing them back neatly inside my suitcase with shiny bright neon colors of purple, pink, and yellow psychedelic circles stripes and squares. It was the kind of luggage usually bought by a grandmother for their pre-school granddaughter during her summer vacation visit. I bought it because I saw it on QVC. There were several other designs in animal prints and a solid color to choose from, but I decided to order the brightest design just because it was the kind of luggage that no one else in their right mind would steal or even buy!

After repacking my luggage, I closed my eyes trying to relax, and soon fell off to sleep. Two hours later, I woke up when my husband, daughter, and grandniece showed up to transport me over to the rehab facility where I was to begin my physical rehabilitation training. I was told the rehab would help me learn how to strengthen my right knee after having a complete knee replacement done one week earlier. I'll never forget that day; it was November 11, 2013. Veterans' Memorial Day-one of the most celebrated days of the year held in the small community where I lived. Many veterans had retired in our town after World War II, Vietnam, and now the Iraq and Afghanistan conflicts. Travis Air Force Base, one of the largest and busiest Air Command stations in the Pacific, was a constant reminder of the many soldiers who lived or died serving our country. I was proud that I was a part of this great military family. As an Air Force wife, I still remember praying for my husband to return safely from Vietnam and Korea on his many assignments to the Far East.

I looked up at my 198lb husband and my tall, beautiful daughter and niece, and I couldn't help but wonder where all of the equipment was the hospital gave me to take with for my rehabilitation, which consisted of:

My electric refrigerated ice pad. The first and only bronze colored walker I'd ever seen. My leg brace to keep my knee in an upright position as I slept. My plastic bag with miscellaneous items and smaller bag inside, with personal items, Lorna Doone cookies, peppermint candy, and mini snicker bars for my late-night snacks.

There was a problem fitting me and three other adults and my extra stuff into the fiery red PT Cruiser. I must have turned the same color when my daughter opened her mouth and said, "Mom, where're we supposed to fit all your stuff?"

I said, "I thought *just* you and Dad were coming to get me?" My husband's sarcastic groan set me on fire. I felt my body temperature rise to hot fury. My face turned as red as my PT Cruiser. I took a deep breath to try to collect my thoughts before I went off on this girl in the calmest tone I managed to say, "There isn't enough room! Why did you bring Kyree (who is my niece) when you knew you were picking me up?"

My daughter's angry stare was disgusting and filled with contempt.

Her dark almond shaped eyes seemed to penetrate through my heart. If I had the power and the strength I once had before surgery, I would have knocked her head off.

"Well, she's going home with me; I already have tickets to take Kyree with me for Veterans' Day weekend."

My head must have spun around twenty times before I could even mutter an incredulous "Oh-really?"

Any other time, I would have been happy for them, but now it felt like I was an old dishrag that they were leaving behind at the doorstep. I tried to figure out-- to visualize my petite 21-year-old niece, and my 200lb. husband stuffed in the back seat. I needed the front seat for my short legs with a brace on it. I would have to sit in the front seat with it pulled all the way back. I said to myself, *"Pearl, just try to keep quiet; remain calm because you don't want your blood pressure to rise."*

Just as I sat down in my wheelchair for the ride out to my car, my daughter announced, "Mom, I have to drop Kyree off at her apartment so she can pack, then I have to pick up Bree (Kyree's sister). Cause they're going to fly back to Denver with me."

Before I could utter a word, a hot fuse went off in my head and up out of my stomach, and up through my throat rose this ugly hot monster spewing out my morning's breakfast of sausage and eggs; I had so proudly kept down for the first time in three days! My daughter and my husband hollered at the same time, "Mom, what did you eat?" I saw their faces frowning with disgust at the sight of food gushing out from within me. My stomach felt like it was caving in and my body went limp. I assured them, I was alright. They insisted on taking my temperature and blood pressure again. The numbers panned out okay after I assured them I would be all right once I got outside in the fresh air.

"I'll go bring the car around 'cause I have got to go pick up Bree!" Off the two ladies scurried leaving me wondering what had happened since last night. There was a definite change in their demeanor from sugary sweet to a sharp sourness since the night before. Dearest daughter had insisted on transporting me from the hospital to the rehab facility.

She told her father, "Daddy, you don't need to pay a shuttle- I'll take Mom!" I insisted, "In case Daddy has some appointments elsewhere, or needs to go somewhere, I wouldn't have to worry; the shuttle will get me there. It's worth the eighty dollars."

My daughter dearest won out in the end. I figured out that she just wanted to do something nice for me.

"No, that's settled. I'll pick you up in the morning. Eighty dollars is too much to spend for that!"

Now, I regretted the decision they made because I felt like I was messing up her plans to be with her younger cousins. My heart ached with pain. I felt my heart freeze as it snapped in two. I closed my eyes hoping to erase the cold uncaring way my own daughter was treating me now.

My dearest husband stayed beside me. With compassion, he asked, "You okay, Shorty?" I simply nodded a yes. Tears flowed down my cheeks. I wiped then quickly away hoping no one saw me.

The nurses who were soon going off shift ran to bring me a bed pan, paper towels, and a wet cold towel to help cool me off. They wiped off my bright emerald green Caftan that a friend (now deceased) had given me. It was from South Africa. I wore the matching scarf, which I proudly tied in African fashion around my head. Now it dangled precariously around my neck like a noose. I tried to fix it but it didn't seem to co-operate. I managed to put it back on my head. The elevator stopped at the first-floor entrance, and the nurses continued pushing me on out the front door while I watched my daughter and my niece scrambling to and from the back seat of the Cruiser, preoccupied with removing fresh crisp MACY'S shopping bags, along with several other bags and new boxes of shoes that were quickly thrown over the back seat to the trunk. I knew I was in for a horrific ride.

She rushed around rearranging their bags from their secret shopping spree in the trunk to fit my luggage into the trunk, Once the trunk was full, Kyree had to hold the other bags in her lap. It confirmed my suspicions of their secret shopping spree at a nearby mall.

I sat in the wheelchair waiting, feeling another wave of nausea rising in up in my stomach. I fought hard to keep it back. I didn't want to ruin their trip. The nurse wheeled me toward the open front door of the car.

My daughter, said, "Oh no, she'll sit in the back, my dad's sitting in the front."

"I'm sitting in the front seat." The nurse assisted me into the front seat. My daughter's dark eyes bore a hole through me. She reached inside the front seat and pulled my seat up as far as she could. Thank God for my short legs, or she could've hurt my injured knee.

I heard a voice saying, "You're so selfish." My husband scowl and deep-seated grumbling caused me to turn around and ask, "Did I hear someone say that I'm selfish?" I turned in time to see my daughter rolling her eyes. "Is there a problem here? Don't let me remind you how selfish I can be from now on."

You can hear a pin drop as she sped off. "Did I need your approval, dear daughter, to sit in my PT Cruiser? In case you two forgot, I just had complete knee replacement and need space to keep my leg straight. After all, this is my car."

Complete silence filled the air as daughter dear spun my car around the circular driveway pushing her foot all the way to the metal in her mad dash to dump me off at the main entrance of rehab facility. My daughter whirred down the Air Base Parkway, turned left quickly onto Walters Road, and then right onto Tabor arriving in less than five minutes into a swerved-curvy driveway, yelling out the window as she let my niece out, "I'll be back after I pick up Bree."

Silently I gave praise and honor to God for keeping me safe with no whiplash injuries despite her reckless driving. I thanked God as I glanced at my cellphone to check the time. It was exactly noon when she pulled into parking lot of the rehab facility. I became dizzy and nauseous from all the swerves and curves of this rollercoaster ride. I thanked God again for getting me there in time for lunch since I had already lost my breakfast.

I had prayed too late or too soon-not sure which-when I felt that same nauseous lump in my stomach rise up and lurch me forward in the car as she stepped on the brake coming to a screeching halt. "Okay Mom, get out now 'Because I've got to get Bree."

After catching my breath, I managed to say, "I 'm not going in there. I'm sick again. Take me home so I can change my clothes."

"No Mom, I'm already late to pick up Bree." She ran toward the automatic double doors yelling back at me, "I'm going in to get someone to bring a wheelchair to take you inside. They'll clean you up."

Just then a staff member ran out. She said, "Is this patient's name Janie Pearl?"

"Yes, it is," my daughter said. "I'm sorry there has been a terrible mix-up. We do not have any vacant beds here. The doctor at David Grant Medical Center insists you drive her back right now."

My daughter was fit to be tied. "What? What kind of rehab facility is this? You mean you don't have a place for her?" She gets back in the front seat and hands me a square plastic container and two white towels while fussing about the place not being professional and unorganized.

I said, "There's a reason for everything. I don't know why, but I'm sure there is something that happened…"

"Well, what kind of place waits until you get there to say that there is no room?"

I continued dry heaving between praying and anointing my car as she sped out of the same circular driveway causing me to vomit even more. I felt hot and my head seemed to spin as I tried to sit up. I felt like I was being punished by her for something, but I had no idea what.

I became furious thinking about my husband who made no objections to the disrespectful way my daughter treated me. I felt like a wet dirty dishrag being thrown away. This was not the man I married who always insisted on his children giving their mother utmost respect. Where was he now? And where was my daughter? I just knew I was in a horrible nightmare. My daughter had never spoken to me like this before. I cried out to Jesus. "Please Lord God take me home!"

The PT Cruiser that I loved was a mess with vomit all over the front dash on the passenger side, and I noticed more on the door as they opened it for me to sit down in the wheelchair. "Oh Mom, hurry and get out, the nurses will take you back inside. I'm not coming in 'Because I'm already late."

I felt as if I would throw up but nothing, but dry heaves wracked my body making me even weaker. The nurses rushed me onto the elevator and back into the same ward where I had left from just thirty minutes earlier. They took my blood pressure and my vitals. I heard someone announce, "Her BP is 201 over 90." I didn't know what it meant, but I knew there were many feet rushing back and forth. I knew several nurses continued working on me. They took my blood pressure every 20 minutes as tears of despair ran down my cheeks. I just didn't want to live anymore. I just wanted to die. I heard my daughter say, "Daddy, come on, let's go."

He said to me, "Call me." No one stayed to see how I was doing, not one of them came over to say goodbye. Did I raise such a monster of a child? Did I ever treat my children this way? A voice spoke to me, "No, you didn't. Fear not my child. You are not going to die. There is still work for you to do."

I didn't know day from night. Nurses came and went on their shifts while I slept. I felt weak and hungry, but I was unable to keep any food down. On the third day, my doctor showed up. He told me how it was divine intervention that brought me back to David Grant Med Center. He explained about the co-coordinator who arranged the transportation and transfer of patients. He said, "Six days ago, the person who coordinated transfers of patients to and from other medical facilities had caught a virus that hospitalized her for six days after showing up at the emergency room.

"She had given the transfer papers to another and thought it had been taken care of. Lucky for you, they didn't have any room for you over at the rehab facility because your blood pressure was extremely high. You were deathly ill. We had to give you blood transfusion and stabilize your blood pressure. I don't know what happened. You were fine when you left here heading over to the Rehab, but something happened to cause your blood pressure to rise to the point of a possible stroke. I don't understand it, but I believe you were saved by a divine intervention. In the many years, I have been on staff here as a physician, this has never happened.

"I'm so glad they did not have a bed for you because they were short staffed for Veterans' Day and by the time, they would've come round to check your vitals, it could have been fatal for you." The doctor asked, "Are you a Christian?" I nodded, yes. "You are truly blessed. It was divine intervention that saved you when you were returned safely back to us."

All I could do was just say, "Thank you Lord for saving me. Oh! The power of the Almighty God." There was purpose in me being tossed and turned up like a salad with too much dressing, from one place to another. I had no idea that the there was a mix up, but thank God there was. If there had been room for me at the other facility, I possibly would have died. But the power of God stepped in and saved me from the grip of death. It just wasn't my time to die.

God spoke to me in the car and told me that I would write this story for just for you. Why was I rejected at one facility, but I was received at another? It was for divine purpose, and to save my life. Many times, we will face rejection through hardships that we cannot figure out. One thing happens after another, and it appears that we are headed in a downward spiral. That's when the hand of God reaches out to us and pulls us up to where He wants us to be. Through this experience, I realized that God is my source. We cannot always depend on others to see or understand what we are going through, because of the sinful and selfish nature of the flesh. God's purpose was revealed to me throughout this horrific event. He wanted me to know that He had me, and that I wasn't going anywhere. He also showed me His power in the process of snatching me right out of the hands of death assigned to my destiny.

You see, I still have a movie to produce that will glorify God and all that He has done in my life. So most definitely my number isn't up. I will do what God has called me to do, just like you!

So the next time you feel as if those who you love have abandoned you like an old dirty dishrag, remember the Lord your God, who gives you the strength to rise out of bed every day of the week. He is your source, and He is your strength. Take your eyes off the frailty of man and set your mind and your heart toward the only true and living God and Savior, who has all power in His hands. Don't allow the circumstances of life to steal your passion from right under your nose, because of what others fail to see in you. You are a direct reflection of your heavenly Father, and He has great plans for you. Be encouraged dear daughter to press toward your purpose, with everything that is within you, and NEVER, EVER give up!

CHAPTER REFLECTIONS:

1. What project have you not finished?
2. When would you like to complete it?
3. How will you reward yourself when you complete it?

Write down your responses to the reflection above in the *Woman of Purpose, Power and Passion Companion Journal*, so that you will have a record of your progress.

Andrea "Michele" Mills

Michele Mills is a published and accomplished author, inspirational speaker, visionary, and entrepreneur. She's the Founder/CEO of *Love In Spite of Women's Bible Fellowship* and she enjoys her coffee business on the side with Oregano Gold.

She has a heart of compassion for the lost and hurting souls. Her message is to inspire and provoke change while speaking the truth in sharing God's word. Her latest project amongst others is to revise *There's Too Much Hell in the Church* and turn it into a musical stage production. A lifelong student of the Word of God, she is continuously furthering her education in theology with an emphasis on biblical studies. Residing in Northern California, she has two children, and two grandchildren.

She's a voice crying in the wilderness "if my people, who are called by my name, will humble themselves and pray and seek my face and turn from their wicked ways, then I will hear from heaven, and I will forgive their sin and will heal their land." 2 Chronicles 7:14

Speaking Engagement & Special Event Contact Information:

Andrea "Michele" Mills

P.O. Box 5447

Oakland, CA 94605

PH: 510-878-8478

Email: Michele_amills@yahoo.com

Web: www.loveinspiteofwomensbiblefellowship.com

CHAPTER FIVE

Chosen Remnant

---

*"No matter how painful the situation
may appear, keep your head UP, God
still cares. We are the apple of His eye."*
-Michele Mills

No, Lord!! It's too painful to share.......

It all started on February 27, 1998.

I am reflecting over my life, searching deep within, and asking the Lord to lead me to any area of my life that would be beneficial to share with girls and young women worldwide to catapult them into their God given purpose. The Lord took me to a place in my past where I blocked out the memory of a painful experience. At this initial revelation I said, "No, Lord! It's too painful to share." For that reason, I said "Lord, are You sure You what me to talk about this?" and He said, "Yes!" He practically confirmed it basically everywhere I went, either through words, people, or places.

I questioned His request simply because I had to go back deep in my past to dig it up and expose the hidden pain. Most of all, I would uncover what I had experienced through the process. Some situations in life can be so heart wrenching, you are thankful when you are past it, but it's not something you want to think about a lot. When we ask the Lord for something, we have to be prepared for His answer. My resolve became regardless of what I experienced, I was willing to be obedient and share my story in hopes that it would help others who may have experienced the same difficulty. Therefore, I started praying and meditating on the matter.

The Holy Spirit reminded me of an important piece of paper in my safe. This safe is locked with a key that I kept on a key ring with all my important keys. I keep all my important papers stored and locked in this miniature sized safe. I located the distinctive key and held it up and glared at it briefly. I ran briskly to get the safe out of the closet and slowly picked it up and then I sat down and put it next to me on the couch. I took the key and opened it. I instantaneously went down memory lane as I quested through and read every piece of significant paper, and low and behold I found it. I read every word on the white petite square piece of paper and then held it.

Headed for Self-Destruction

It was back in my thirties, a time when I was not committed to Lord, but I had certain values that I stood by, one. I was married at this time, living life aimlessly my way, and certainly headed for self-destruction. My second marriage was on the rocks, and sadly my husband and I knew it. We were not really paying attention to each other's needs or actions toward one another. One day, I was feeling sick to my stomach, the aroma of food was making me nauseous. I thought to myself, "Hmm I've felt this way before," instead of assuming, I took a home pregnancy test. It was positive, and I said, "No, this can't be," especially not at this age or time in my life.

Everything possible appeared to be going wrong. Still in denial, I decided to go to the doctor. It was February 27, 1998. I remember waiting in the doctor's office for my name to be called so I could take another pregnancy test. I truly thought I was dreaming, and I could not believe I let myself get into this situation. I began to pray and beg the Lord, "Please Lord, don't let me be pregnant." Well, it was finally my turn to go in. I took the test and waited for the results. The nurse gave me a piece of paper with the results, and it indicated I was four weeks and one day pregnant and my expected due date was December 3, 1998.

For a moment, I was saddened, and then suddenly, I was instantly happy. I got into the car and started driving towards home and I began visualizing having another baby to provide and care for. I told my husband, children, friends, and some family members. My husband tried to be happy about it, and of course, I could understand we were not in a good place in our relationship.

Our marriage was in chaos and quite frankly, it was not getting any better. I knew that other activities away from home were taking his attention as well as mine. Still, I started settling and preparing in my mind for a new child. I started thinking on names for a girl or boy. I started getting excited. For some reason, I felt it was a girl, and I was going to name her Angela.

One day I got the surprise of my life, and was hit with these words, "We are not going to be together." I knew deep within that he was right. However, I could not believe our discussion shifted from not being together to talking about me having an abortion. This idea hit me hard, for the simple fact that I was against abortion. Everybody knew my position on abortion because I had spoken it; I thought I would never have one, no matter what. Now, here I was faced with it. Sometimes we don't know how deeply we believe something until it is tested. I felt so perplexed. How could I tell my family and friends that I am having an abortion, or better yet, how could I face God? I needed someone to talk to quickly. I could not shake the words "We are not going to be together." Hence, I reached out and I discussed the issue on having an abortion with one of my dear friends at the time. She said, "You can't! It's not you." I said, "I know," but, my husband is right, we are not going to be together, and I already have two children. I can't do this alone, I just can't. At that moment, whatever faith I did still have was all gone. I was walking in fear.

The enemy was tormenting my mind with all sorts of thoughts. Such as: "You can't have another child alone. How is you going to provide? You already have two children. You are too old; your baby might be born disabled." I could not bear it. My mind was set on the abortion; on the other hand, I needed help to go through with it. So, I began drinking heavily and getting high to try and cope and not to think about what I was about to do.

My husband went with me to proceed with the abortion. We arrived at the abortion clinic, and I remember us waiting to be called, I was scared and very nervous. I wanted to run out. I said, "Lord, do something to stop this from taking place." My name was finally called. I got up at a snail's pace and walked into the room. I remember taking off my clothes, putting on a gown, getting up on a bed, opening my legs, putting my feet into the gurney, and still praying to God to help me, and intervene somehow. Even though we must deal with the consequences of our own actions, and take responsibility, I was still expecting a miracle, and hoping God would intervene.

It was time, the nurse came in and chatted with me for a moment, tears filled my eyes as she proceeded. She gave me a shot to put me to sleep, when I woke up it was over. I did not remember anything that took place. Nonetheless I did not feel right. However, spiritually, I was feeling shameful and guilty. Physically, I was experiencing lower abdominal pain, and without delay, I thought something was wrong. I sincerely thought God was about to punish me, and I asked the nurse was the way I was feeling normal after such a procedure. She said I should be okay and recommended that I return to the clinic if the pain persisted after a couple of days.

After the abortion was over, I had the audacity to be angry with God, and I wasn't even in right standing with Him. Still, I was seriously angry. Extreme notion, I was expecting him to intervene, in some sort of way and He did not. The reality was God was there but I, my husband, my mother, and one of my dear friends were the only ones who knew about the abortion. I told everyone else I had a miscarriage, simply because I was ashamed and I could not say the word "abortion," not me, the woman who stood against it for years. I could not believe I had killed by baby. It was difficult to handle. I stayed in the bed crying and drinking for weeks, it appeared everything around me, had to do with a baby. It was the mother walking down the street with her newborn baby or a friend announcing her pregnancy and the countless TV commercials that all seemed to feature babies. My world was falling apart.

My husband comforted me for a while. He catered to my every need. Surprisingly, it momentarily brought us closer, we even cried together. It appeared that he was able to get over it much quicker and carry on than I was able to. To this day, I don't think he truly knew or understood the pain I was feeling deep inside. I could not stop thinking about my baby.

I felt so ashamed and in so much pain. It got to the point where I just did not want to live. I remember clear as day, on one dreadful morning, sitting Indian style on my California King waterbed, crying, and thinking about my life and the precious life that I took, by taking matters into my own hands, as opposed to trusting and believing God would work things out for the good. I did not want to live any more. I started pondering suicide, even to the point of writing a note to my two children; I was in a very selfish state. While thinking about how I was going to end my life, I heard a loud voice outside my window saying, "God still cares!" I jumped off my bed and looked out the window, and I saw a man walking up the street; he looked back, smiled and kept on walking. I knew he was an angel from the Lord. The entire atmosphere in my room changed, and I felt the presence of God...I started weeping and crying. I cried out, "Thank you, Lord Jesus!!!" I knew then, as always, I was chosen to do a work for the Lord.

My Journey to Grace

Even though it doesn't give grounds for an abortion, my husband was correct about us; we divorced within a year after the abortion. My children and I moved out-of- state. I remember on the bus thinking back over my life and praying to God for a new start. I recall at a rest stop; my daughter passed me a book from the bookshelf in one of the stores. It was titled, *If Momma Ain't Happy, Ain't Nobody Happy.* Those words stayed with me as we finally arrived at our destination, Georgia. Praise God my desire for drugs and alcohol was completely gone. I buried the thought of having an abortion as though it never happened. Most importantly, I repented and rededicated my life back to Lord and my new journey began. I started working on a temporary assignment at *Coca-Cola Company* and attending church. My life was filled with quality time with the Lord, and reading and meditating on His word, and with fasting and praying. We spent a great deal of time walking and talking together on this five-mile trail I walked daily.

Several months later, I sensed the Lord was telling me it's time to move back to California. Therefore, I started praying and asking the Lord for confirmation. After a period and many confirmations to move back home, to name a few, my first confirmation was given on a Sunday morning. Surprisingly it was my first prophetic word given by a woman, as I was walking in the parking lot on my way to my car to leave church, she said, "I have a word for you. The Lord has equipped you, and it is time to go home." I glared at her with amazement, mind you, I had never been prophesied over, nor had I ever experienced or heard of such a thing. When I arrived back to my car, I sat there in wonder and my eyes filled with tears of joy.

Thereafter, the Lord kept giving me confirmation after confirmation to return home. My last confirmation; I was fasting and praying and seeking the Lord for one final word and the Holy Spirit spoke, "Go home happy." I started packing my clothes and received a phone call for an interview in San Francisco. I arrived at San Francisco and got the job. During the time that I was in Georgia that the Lord gave me the scripture,

"Trust in the Lord with all thy heart and lean not to thy own understanding, and all thy ways acknowledge Him and He shall direct thy paths." Proverbs 3:5-6 (KJV)

I made so many decisions based on my way of thinking, therefore, I made a commitment to the Lord, I would try to pray, seek Godly council and confirmation to do things His way before stepping out.

Many Are Called but Few Are Chosen

So, I ended up back in California, and the Lord told me to get active in ministry. It will lead you to your divine purpose and help with accountability. This goes to show us, no matter what we have experienced, or bad decisions we may have made, God is gracious and merciful to His children. He has a deep compassion. He is a God of love. For that reason, He doesn't love us because we do everything right; He loves us because He is love. It's His nature and He has a wonderful perfect plan for our lives.

"I beseech you therefore, brethren, by the mercies of God, that you present your bodies a living sacrifice, holy, acceptable to God, which is your reasonable service. And do

not be conformed to this world, but be transformed by the renewing of your mind, that you may prove what is that good and acceptable and perfect will of God." Romans 12:1-2 (NKJV)

Therefore, I immersed myself into ministry and began to serve in various departments such as single's director, youth media manager, convalescent ministry, evangelism team, women's ministry, new members' department, and children's director. In the interim in serving in different capacities in the church, I felt the Holy Spirit calling me into ministry. It was in the year 2000, and He gave me two scriptures:

"The Spirit of the Lord GOD is upon me; because the LORD hath anointed me to preach good tidings unto the meek; he hath sent me to bind up the brokenhearted, to proclaim liberty to the captives, and the opening of the prison to them that are bound; To proclaim the acceptable year of the LORD, and the day of vengeance of our God; to comfort all that mourn; To appoint unto them that mourn in Zion, to give unto them beauty for ashes, the oil of joy for mourning, the garment of praise for the spirit of heaviness; that they might be called trees of righteousness, the planting of the LORD, that he might be glorified. And they shall build the old wastes, they shall raise up the former desolations, and they shall repair the waste cities, the desolations of many generations. And strangers shall stand and feed your flocks, and the sons of the alien shall be your plowmen and your vinedressers. But ye shall be named the Priests of the LORD:

men shall call you the Ministers of our God: ye shall eat the riches of the Gentiles, and in their glory shall ye boast yourselves. For your shame ye shall have double; and for confusion they shall rejoice in their portion: therefore in their land they shall possess the double: everlasting joy shall be unto them. " Isaiah 61:1-7 (KJV)

"And he gave some, apostles; and some, prophets; and some, evangelists; and some, pastors and teachers; For the perfecting of the saints, for the work of the ministry, for the edifying of the body of Christ. " Ephesians 4:11-12 (KJV*)*

I made an appointment to meet with my pastor, and he confirmed the call. He directed me to start taking "ministers in training" classes. Thereafter, the Lord called me to the prayer ministry, and I joined the prayer team at my church. He would relentlessly wake me up at 5:00am to pray, read His word and spend intimate time with Him. So, daily, I'd get up at 5:00am and brew some delicious Folgers coffee and pour it in my cup and sup with the Lover of my soul. He would speak through scripture and through my spirit; we have such precious moments and memories. As a result, prayer has become a lifestyle for me. He then started waking me up at 3:33am, which led me to Jeremiah 3:33,

"Call to me and I will answer you and show you great and mighty things, fenced in and hidden, which you do not know. " This has become one of my favorite scriptures.

My family and friends were happy I was substance free; however, they did not understand my addiction, for the lover of my soul, my keeper, my friend, my, everything, my Lord and Savior Jesus Christ. Some felt I was acting a little peculiar, which I was, and was so happy about it.

"Believers collectively are set apart for God and his kingdom as a 'holy nation and to proclaim the gospel of salvation to his glory and praise'" (*Life in the Spirit Study Bible Commentary*).

As the Lord was working in my life spiritually, He led me to start my own business. I stepped out on faith and started my own childcare business. It was Christian, had low rates, and opened for 24 hours, and provided transportation service. Praise God I was able to be a light to so many families. The Lord blessed tremendously.

While running my childcare, I was attending full-time bible college taking day and night classes. I received my certification in biblical and urban studies and later received my minister's license from the church I was attending at the time. After praying and seeking confirmation, I closed my childcare in 2005. I sensed the Lord was leading me to full time ministry.

The Lord would continuously show me a flock of birds flying with one bird in the front leading the flock. I knew He was calling me to pastor a church and start a women's ministry. However, I did not fill the release to pastor yet. So, I went with the women's ministry and started the process with my 501c, and launched *Love Inspite of Women's Bible Fellowship.* We met at my home for Bible study, prayer and food. The Lord gave me this scripture,

"And they continued steadfastly in the apostles' doctrine and fellowship, in the breaking of bread, and in prayers. Then fear came upon every soul, and many wonders and signs were done through the apostles. Now all who believed were together, and had all things in common, and sold their possessions and goods, and divided them among all, as anyone had need. So continuing daily with one accord in the temple, and breaking bread from house to house, they ate their food with gladness and simplicity of heart, praising God and having favor with all the people. And the Lord added to the church daily those who were being saved." Acts 2:42-47 (KJV)

While running my non-profit organization, the Lord had me continue to serve in different churches.

He's a moving God

I transitioned to a new church home, and the Holy Spirit led me to serve in the prison ministry and to be trained in the Prophetic Institute; this was something very new to me. However, I was blessed beyond measure with ministering to the women in Santa Rita Jail. I went in to bless and came out blessed and filled with so much joy.

There were certain traits I possessed that I didn't understand, but the Prophetic Institute brought clarity to the characteristics the Lord placed within me. As a result, I believe every church that's operating in the five-fold ministry needs a Prophetic Institute. There are so many people in the Body of Christ operating in the prophetic that need training and coaching, especially in order, and most importantly, knowing when to release a word from the Lord.

When the Lord gives us a word, we need to pray for his timing to release it. He may want us to keep it in secret to pray over until He gives us the release to share it. He needs to know; He can trust us. In other words, we need His wisdom. We want to pray for a pure flow of the prophetic, too many tainted words are spoken over God's people. We need to stop getting caught up in the hype, so we can distinguish the flesh from the spirit…Just saying!!!!

Not only was the Lord teaching and building me up in the prophetic, but He was also leading me to write. My first writing project was part of an anthology, *Victorious Living for Women*. My chapter was entitled, *"I've Got the Victory."* I shared my testimony without including my abortion and it blessed my soul and others. I was able to release to get to the next chapter of my journey.

Another work I was released to write is *There's Too Much Hell in the Church*. This book is about different scenarios I experienced in the church or some scenarios that others may have shared with me. I praise God for giving me the courage to finish it. Many people weren't happy with the title or content mainly because it exposed some of the wickedness within the Body. However, there were many people who were blessed by it.

Fortunately, they were able to see themselves in certain situations I was led to share. After reading it repeatedly, and recently reading it again after three years in the making, I know it was God leading me to be a ready writer for Him. Sadly, if anything, the book is even more pertinent today for some of the churches across America. Praise the Lord! He is leading me to revise and turn *There's Too Much Hell in the Church* into a musical stage production. I also thank God for two other anthologies, *Keeping the Faith* and *Victorious Living for Moms*.

My long-term goal is to open a transitional house for women and children. I thank and praise God for giving me the opportunity to be house coordinator for a transitional home for women. In my one year, I learned a great deal living there and serving. I am ever so grateful for the opportunity. I know without a shadow of doubt, with all my experiences throughout my journey in the church and Christendom, the Lord will work it together for His good according to His purpose. I thank God for what He is preparing me for the next stage of my journey. I truly believe He's releasing me to pastor. This is His divine purpose. Stay Tuned!!!

Chosen Remnant

No matter what we may have experienced, God knew us before the foundation of the world, He knew us when we were in our mother's womb. We are fearfully and wonderfully made.

"I will praise You for I am fearfully and wonderfully made; Marvelous are Your works, And that my soul knows very well." Psalm 139:14 (NKJV)

We are a peculiar people, set apart for the Master's use. Don't worry if you don't fit in -- worry when you do fit in. Always remember we are royalty, a holy nation, we are called, chosen. We are not merely chosen to be just a light, but we are chosen to be a marvelous light. Wherever we go, we should shine brightly. Why? Because He called us out of darkness into His marvelous light.

1 Peter 2:9 & 10 states, *"But ye are a chosen generation, a royal priesthood, an holy nation, a peculiar people; that ye should shew forth the praises of him who hath called you out of darkness into his marvelous light; Which in time past were not a people, but are now the people of God: which had not obtained mercy, but now have obtained mercy."* (KJV)

Many are called but few are chosen. There's a cost to following the Lord: will you draw back, or will you keep pressing toward the mark, no matter what? Count the cost, *"And whoever does not carry their cross and follow me cannot be my disciple. Suppose one of you wants to build a tower. Won't you first sit down and estimate the cost to see if you have enough money to complete it?"* Luke 14:27-28 (AMP)

I thank God for leading me to participate in this anthology. It's been 16 years since my abortion, and I hadn't been led to share. I know now with God, there's a timing to share certain portions of our testimony. I believe He wants our heart to be right and assured we can handle it being fully released. It has certainly set me free in an area I kept hidden, while still moving forward and serving the Lord. It was painful at first, especially after digging and re-opening a wound that has not completely healed.

I am a firm believer in the need to release everything that could possibly hinder the Lord from taking us to greater levels in Him. We need to release and let go of everything buried deep within us. I am a witness! Thank you, Lord Jesus, for your perfect timing!

His Great Grace

In closing, for any girl or young woman who is faced with making a choice for abortion, seek Godly counsel and trust God for all your fears. He will see you through.

"Where no counsel is, the people fall: but in the multitude of counsellors there is safety." Proverbs 11:14 (NKJV)

And for any girl or young woman who may have had an abortion, my chapter is to hopefully inspire and remind you that we serve a forgiving God, and He knows our pain better than anyone else. The Lord Jesus Christ hates the sin, but He loves the sinner.

After true godly repentance, we need to seek the Lord in helping forgive ourselves. The enemy is the one who wants to keep us living in shame and condemnation, so we can't move forward freely in God.

"There is therefore now no condemnation for those who are in Christ Jesus. For the law of the Spirit of life has set you free in Christ Jesus from the law of sin and death." Romans 8:1-2 (ESV).

Everyone's process is different. The Lord dealt with me in a supernatural way. My deliverance was quick, simply because of what He was calling me to do; therefore, I was able to bury the abortion and was freed immediately from the substance abuse. I thank God for His great grace.

"He said to me, My grace (My favor and loving-kindness and mercy) is enough for you [sufficient against any danger and enables you to bear the trouble manfully]; for My strength and power are made perfect (fulfilled and completed) and show themselves most effective in [your] weakness. Therefore, I will all the more gladly glory in my weaknesses and infirmities, that the strength and power of Christ (the Messiah) may rest (yes, may pitch a tent over and dwell) upon me!" 2 Corinthians 12:9-11 *(AMP)*

I am now freed from my past and able to tell my entire testimony without shame or guilt. My past has been erased by the blood of Jesus. I am completely new in Christ. *"Therefore, from now on, we regard no one according to the flesh. Even though we have known Christ according to the flesh, yet now we know Him thus no longer. Therefore, if anyone is in Christ, he is a new creation; old things have passed away; behold, all things have become new."* 2 Corinthians 5:16-17 (KJV)

Here's My Prayer

Father God, I come boldly before your throne of grace entering your gates with thanksgiving and praise. Thank you for loving us despite our shortcomings, thank you for your unconditional love, thank you for your loving kindness. For you are an awesome God, and there's no other like you, you are worthy to be praised.

Your loving-kindness is better than life. For you are the King of kings, the Lord of lords, the Alpha and Omega, the Beginning, and the End, the First and the Last. You are a Mighty God, and we worship you alone. In the name of Jesus!

Father God, I come lifting every girl, every woman, and every person that's reading this chapter of my life. I pray you would touch them in a supernatural way, I pray their inner being is strengthened by your divine words. I pray you would renew their minds with the mind of Christ and their way of thinking. For your Word says,

"Finally, brethren, whatsoever things are true, whatsoever things are honest, whatsoever things are just, whatsoever things are pure, whatsoever things are lovely, whatsoever things are of good report; if there be any virtue, and if there be any praise, think on these things." Philippians 4:8

I pray they would learn to trust and lean on you in all their ways and lean not to their own understanding…I pray they would stand strong in you. In the name of Jesus!

Father God, I come against every foul spirit, every unclean spirit, every demonic spirit, and every spirit of depression, every spirit of fear, every spirit of death, and every spirit that's not like you, Lord Jesus. I come against it right now, in the mighty name of Jesus!

I decree and declare we are free and loosed to flow completely in You. Have your way, Holy Spirit.

We thank you in advance for what you are about to do. In Jesus name, I pray. Amen!

CHAPTER REFLECTION:

1. What does forgiveness look like?

2. What does restoration look like?

3. What does grace look like?

Write your responses to the above reflection in the *Woman of Purpose, Power and Passion Companion Journal*; to remind you of your personal commitment to yourself, to empower someone else through your experiences.

Dr. Lakita D. Long

Dr. Lakita D. Long is an inspiring motivational/spiritually empowering individual, who is totally engaged in helping people change their life. She concentrates on speaking with a purpose until her audience, have their own thinking out loud moment, giving life-long tools to both men and women. As a speaker, author, educator, life consultant, social therapist, radio host and coach, she focuses her energies around providing relevant information to help transform the lives of children, youth, women, and families. With her book, *Change Your Life: The 90 Day Experience*, she has helped women across the country learn that change only happens when what you know is no longer good enough and has made them a believer in their own dreams. She wanted to make sure that women understood the power of their personal 'yes,' and how to build momentum from ground zero. As the author of *Starting Over and Loving It* allows her to share how you move forward with nothing in your hands! Dr. Lakita is commonly known as the people's therapist; she loves using biblical principles and psychological concepts to help individuals better engage their life.

As the founder and driving force behind *InspiringYou Ministries, GodIsTheBusiness.com, Inc., Change Your Life Seminars, Inspiring You Global Enterprises, LLC*, and a participator in many *Think Tanks and Strategy Brainstorm Consortiums* across the country. Lakita has embraced the calling on her life and has stepped into the forefront of changing the lives of others as she lives out her God given destiny to impact the world by *Speaking with A Purpose.*

With educational training and degrees in psychology, counseling, and doctorate training and degrees in counseling psychology and social psychology, she shares her message based on her conviction, experience, and research enabling people to "Think Outloud" and give them permission to live a life worth living. She is a woman living on purpose in real time!

Speaking Engagement & Special Event Contact Information:

Dr. Lakita D. Long
P.O. Box 3902
Antioch, CA 94531
PH: 925-238-8711
Email: Lakita@LakitaLong.org
Web: www.LakitaLong.org

CHAPTER SIX

Within Myself: Finding the Real ME

---

*"Anytime someone is able to be free in
their mind, body and soul, it resurrects
the natural glow in their life."*
—Dr. Lakita Long

How many of you have ever been in a situation where someone asked you to do something and truly you didn't want to do it but because you didn't want to say no, or get the response after your no, you did it anyway? The one thing I'm sure you were not aware of at that time, was how this one little gesture could alter and shape your life forever and create much turmoil later in life. At least it did for me.

Growing up in a semi-impoverished family with so many secrets, so much mishandling of one's another's trust, where there were seven siblings, a great amount of frustration, and a breakdown of the family system it was easy to adopt someone's thoughts about me and exclude how I really felt. In many of your homes, or growing up, your family was probably like mine in some instance. I am number 6 out of 7 children and the youngest girl. I have a younger brother, and although our siblings are older than we were, they still lingered around the house, and just too many times there was no privacy, boundaries were always crossed, yet there was a high level of secrecy, all of which in psychological terms describes enmeshment.

Trying to find myself, the true Lakita, in a home filled with enmeshment, living with lies and secrets, and a heart that was divided within was virtually impossible. Always presenting a public appearance, but never revealing the private reality of who I was.

Enmeshment is a concept that merely describes when a person becomes way too involved in someone else's issues to the point that they lose their own essence, or it never fully develops. This phenomenon goes cross-culturally and breaks down many socio-economic barriers. Because of all of this, when it was time to stand up and be me, I just couldn't. Other people's thought and what they thought about me plagued my life as a child and did not stop until I was a teenager. It was then that I learned that sometimes, when we are lost within ourselves, only the one who created us could help us come out again.

Living this way made me think so negatively of myself. I really hated who I was and said it constantly within my own soul and spirit. I took an eraser and etched my initials on my hand (ouch) when I was just 10 years old. The mark is still there on my right hand. This was just the beginning of the self-injurious behavior all because I was "within myself" and did not know who I really was.

As I got older, my concern was going to be about the way I saw myself, and essentially others, trying to protect that negative self-image that I built up, while being this very depressed, dangerous person within. You see, most high achievers struggle with something from their past, and if not dealt with kills their future. I am so grateful that I began working on the issues that I saw plague me early on, so that I would only have the victory to talk about. But the struggle was very real, which is why I want to talk about it to help somebody who is negative, depressed, and self-injurious within.

I am not sure what caused me to think so negative of myself, and that life was not worth living, *unless I was doing something to please people.* I sense that it was the fear of not being able to please individuals properly and that they would reject me totally, and that frightened me. It overwhelmed me to the point that I would self-predict that people were not going to like something that I was doing or saying. It hindered me wanting to learn more about myself, and I became consumed about everyone else.

I loved the response, the applause, and the feeling that I was loved. I was so into helping others look great and be great that I was living this out in both conscious and unconscious realms. This was what my teenage years and early and early adulthood reflected. To many people in my neighborhood, my public appearance displayed a bright, talented, flamboyant young kid with lots of energy, but had no place to express it. The private person inside was dying to be heard for just being herself.

While many thought I was the intelligent prodigy of my family, they failed to realize how many problems I had, and never asked me how I felt. I had so many issues that literally almost destroyed my life. Being molested by a woman when I was 8 years old, who was a family friend, having random "hump" experiences with boys in the neighborhood, and everyone thinking that I was "fast"! Getting date raped at the age of 14 years old and going back to the person who did it because I wanted to make the offense go away and offer myself to him only to be humiliated again. I later learned that he died of AIDS when I was in college. But the grace of God spared me. I would make others think I was so strong and levelheaded when most of the time I was a weak child. I was trying to live up to various standards, lost my childhood and un-bagged a world of guilt, shame, pride and arrogance.

It is imperative to understand your motives behind doing things, for I can remember doing things in elementary, not because I wanted to, but because that was something that I should do to win the approval of others. I would enter singing contests because people told me I should, but I didn't truly care to do that. So henceforth throughout the years everything I did was with many misconstrued motives that often was very different from my private reality.

I want to go back a moment to talk about my growing up. As a child I learned about what pleases people and makes them happy. When my mother and father would have house parties, I would get in the middle of the floor and start dancing. This was a ritualistic thing. But I only did it because people asked me to, so while the attention was on me rarely did, I truly receive the attention I needed to make me an emotionally stable child. Because of this type of activity, I learned that to be noticed, appreciated, and loved, you had to do something. You could not just be present because in my social world, only those who were in the forefront got noticed and applauded with accolades. This began my tireless effort to be the best at everything and be in everything. This by itself is just totally exhausting.

When you spend all your time trying to secure the attention of others, you will no doubt experience a lack of self-care, a lack of self-respect, neglect of self, and hatred towards others. My early remembrance of rejection came about because people including my parents and siblings seemed to be only interested in what I could do, but not who I was. At least that is how I felt and saw things. When it was about school, achievement or something like that then I felt like I had their attention, but other things like learning how to be a better young girl, or like an eternal case of mental internal wars I was labeled, but not helped. They would say you are too hyper, too evil; you are mean, I don't trust you, or you lie too much. But then on another level they were telling all the people how great I was… so confusing. So, one minute

I loved myself, but the next minute I hated myself and at any given time I allowed suicidal thoughts to pervade my thinking. So you say, you were pathologically disturbed, and you are probably right according to today's mental health definition. But was I really, or just a kid frustrated with life's circumstances and using everything in life to act as a defensive measure to uphold a false image. Was I trying to tell others that I was being secretly sexually handled by the neighborhood boys, or that older men were trying to seduce me in their bedrooms? Should I have been given a shot of Ritalin for all my outbursts in class, intense level of hyperactivity, and unruly disciplinary actions? Or would taking the medicine make my life worse off than it really was?

I am sure that if I had to take Ritalin or any of the other ridiculous drugs on the market to cure a child's behavioral level, it would have only added to the rest of my stigmas and would have truly singled me out. Because even as a young child, I knew that the teachers in elementary could not keep quiet about anything, and it would be throughout the entire school. The reason why I am focusing currently on the elementary years of my life is because I want to accurately show you a developmental phase of actions and activities, which lead later, lead to ill-psychotic thought patterns as a teenager.

As a child I never knew what it meant to love myself. I never saw how true love was supposed to be, and that you don't degrade yourself to get it. I could not replicate it to anyone or myself. I knew that my brothers, sisters, mother, and father didn't love themselves because they allowed themselves to be controlled by alcohol, other abusive substances, as well as by other people. At times I would sit and rationalize with myself about what I should give myself permission to do. I would search for approval for everything to be okay with my decisions and wanted to be needed by others. I never realized how much people controlled my spirit and caused me not to stand up on my own. A prime example of this was when I was 14 years old and I liked a guy who was 23 years old, a drug dealer who had two babies by two different women. The fact that it looked like he had some interest in me was enough to lower my standards and talk about sex and other perverse things over the phone, not knowing that just a few weeks after the conversation, I would be a victim of date rape. He simply took advantage of me, and because I did not know what it meant to say no, I lay there frozen in disbelief, and drowned in my tears, which developed from the guilt and shame of thinking that things would be different. He even had the nerve to tell me that I was too small (speaking of my vagina) and that I was not ready, and he was the one that was going to make me ready. Imagine where my self-esteem went. The little girl inside of me was crying for help. While I continued to struggle to find myself, I was drawn to the Spirit of God. But I still battled with being date raped and many other issues for another year and a half.

Although I had been going to church since I was 4 years old, it wasn't until the Lord filled me with the Holy Spirit at age 12 that I notice that yes, I am different, but different doesn't mean bad. Even after my conversion and experience of having a relationship with God, I still went through a lot of things. I still had to deal with my insecurities about being accepted, even though I know that I was accepted by God. I had to keep running to God to help me deal with my interactions with men, because I did not know what interactions with men were supposed to look like.

I really wanted to share a tidbit about the struggle of living within myself, because I know that many people today in their thirties and forties are struggling to find themselves, because of earlier things in their life. I was greatly fortunate with a variety of turns of events in my life, in which God helped me. Self-hatred was a drug, and I was no good for many years, unless I had a shot of it every day. And if things were good, it made me nervous, and I would sabotage the experience so that it reflected my self-fulfilled prophecy that I was not good enough.

Although this story sounds like many other people's story, truly the difference is the recovery of my mind. You do not feel okay simply by wanting to feel okay; you must war for the parts of you that have been carelessly given over to something or someone else.

I decided to write about "within myself" because I can tell by people's speech and interaction now as older individuals that they are struggling with the exact same thing, but the difference is that they have not dealt with it yet. Even when you come to the knowledge of Christ/God, it does not go away immediately. I got my deliverance when I was 15 years old, but I fought for 7 years after for the fullness of wholeness. I understand why it took so long to get to that place, but it was painful. Constantly battling within you, when you were always fine from the beginning, I just didn't know that fully.

The Child within Each of Us

Each of us has a little child that cries out every now and then to have fun or just do something that is great. And it is important for children to find that part in their life. What I mean about a child being inside of you is that there is a part of us that wishes to remain naïve and cuddly and revert to those days of youthfulness. For me, my childhood was stripped away, as are so many other children in the inner city, and it took a very long time to rebuild and gain the things that were lost simply because I raised myself. The same could also be true for those who grew up in affluent families, because they are taught a lot of adult things at a young age and was sometimes not given the choice to learn it, you just had to be it.

When you are a child and you are given the responsibility to "hustle" up money to help pay for rent, or get food, or buy your school clothes, it changes the way you operate in that family. How you see and feel about yourself changes (a prostitute in exchange for love), and you just see things different, sometimes just off. Because I started reading when I was 3 years old, I read as you could imagine a lot of things that I had no business reading. Thus began my fascination to porn induced books, books about magic, mystery, and death began to be my only interests.

My addiction to reading about sex and the like would create a spirit in me that I did not know others could see and thought that I wanted what they saw. This sexually overt young girl, who would speak like what she read in the books, only to have to back up her words, found herself in bad situations.

Through much prayer, was I able to get this young child redirected to her rightful place, but I had to go deep within myself and find the real me.

Transitioning to the Real Me

When I finally came to terms with the fact that the way I was living and being as a teenager up until age 21 or so, I knew that I could not live that way forever. As a matter of fact, it started to interrupt the plans that I knew that God had for me. When you make the solemn decision to be bigger and better than you ever have, you must make the transition to the real you. I speak a lot about this process because I believe in it wholeheartedly. So many individuals have lost the desire to even find that real person, and others spend their entire lives frustrated because they know they are not that real person.

This is the hardest part of living to me. You must look within yourself, and give a deep sigh, with a desire to do something about what is going on in your psyche, and your heart. I was divided within to either do what people thought I should do, or what I knew that I was called to. The moment that I started fully branching out, was the moment that I started transitioning to the real me.

When I got to UC Berkeley as a 17-year-old freshman, pre-law major, and on the fast track to become a corporate attorney, I did about 2 semesters of the classes that helped me to declare majors for law school stuff, and realized, I must be true to me. I like to help people, and deal with the matters of their heart and mind, and I was not going to be able to do that as an attorney. I am passionate about helping people with their mental health issues, speaking, advocating and training on what is necessary to help others become well again in their thinking. Even though I made the shift in college, it would still be 2 years as a student that I would even tell my family that I switched from pre-law to psychology. Finally, I came to terms with the fact that I have to live a life that is authentic to me, and that I was going to be happy about. Now the time to transition to the real me was evident.

While this transitioning time is not easy, it is a necessity to have your full mind intact, and joy in your heart. Most of people's frustrations and heaviness is due to the residue and consistency of living the aspirations and dreams of someone else. It is time that you transition, move onward into a different space and place, and encounter the real you again. When I finally came to myself, I forgot how funny I was, because I lived in the realm of seriousness for so long, that laughter and joy were foreign to me. I am so glad for the transition.

Being Free to Be You

You have never imagined how hard it would be to be you, until the day you tried. All your life, you've sat around idealizing other people's life, and tried to live yours through theirs, or you let them live their lives through yours. These escalating events caused you to be enslaved to the spirit of emulation. Anytime someone can be free in their mind, body and soul, it resurrects the natural glow in their life, which is why it is so important to being free to be you. We live in such a masked society, where even in the place that you are okay to be yourself (church), we hide in the religiosity of spirituality and we lose the natural vitality of growth, and freedom. When I finally was free to be me, I shined even brighter, and remembered that I had that same shine when I was younger. But after the constant ill spoken words that I started believing, I allowed others to dim my shine. I promise you, being free to be you, is the best thing that can ever happen to you.

When you make this decision and look within, you will find as I did that your focus is to learn to understand the true you. This will probably have you going through an identity crisis, but you will survive that.

Going through the Identity Crisis Process

When you start going through the identity crisis process, several things will happen. First you will feel awkward in everything you do. Why? Remember you have lived your life based on what others thought you should do, and inadvertently you did it, so you don't know what it feels like to be really you. You will feel incompetent, and you will recollect lots of negative experiences in your life. As I did, I couldn't believe that I was freely being me, so it started to feel weird. But by then I had enough of "feeling good" to know that I wanted to stay on that side, and I just pressed beyond the feelings to go back being someone else.

Some of the dysfunction that I experienced and that many people experience is due to the constant identity crisis they keep going through because they live in constant fear of others seeing the real person. I often tell people that you must do stuff without the fear of what others think and/or will say. I know you think that you don't care what others say about you, but the truth of the matter is that you do care.

119

I cared for far too long, and it almost cost me my life. I remember one time someone saying something cruel and negative to me in junior high. My friends thought I should have been more hostile or showed that I was bothered by the other person's actions. Sadly, I didn't know how to express myself because I was so used to being embarrassed, humiliated, and it just didn't register how I should properly respond. I later started acting like I was really upset with the person, but I wasn't angry at all. I just pretended to be so that my friends wouldn't think I was stupid.

So, once you go through your time of identity and going back and forth, you will deal with the fear element of staying true to yourself. Transitioning out of fear is tough when you have lived fearfully most of your life.

Transitioning out of fear

Fear is the one element that perpetuates itself. It can reenergize itself, without a whole lot of interaction from you. All it needs is just a second of your inner thoughts, and it will begin to torment you for days if you let it. Fear has had so much fun in my life, until I realized it was not a great partner to have around. Fear brought depression, and everything looked bleak. This part of the process of looking "within myself" really hurt, because I felt like I was going through bouts of shock treatment. As soon as I had my heart and mind set on being free from the entanglement of fear, I would become scared, isolated, and tormented. The cycle continued to perpetuate until I realized that fear fed my existence as well as the lies about myself that I bought into. The same is true for you. You must recognize fear, but you don't have to embrace its impact. You should only focus on fear to get clear about the truth of it all and do something different.

We were not created to live a life of fear, because it robs us of the creative ability to do what God has called us to do in the earth. When fear is allowed to remain, gives us the illusion that we cannot do certain things that we have already been given the power to do. It is so important to move out of the place of fear and get completely sober in our thinking about our reality so that we have the freedom to thrive in God and for God. What you must do is recognize fear and refuse to embrace it. If you continue to hold on to it, it will leave your life as dry as dead men's bones, and as brittle as a day-old cracker. You are always looking for someone else to validate the essence that should be strong in you, but fear has covered your natural strength.

You have the power to transition out of fear! But if you choose to remain in fear, you will remain in the realm of depression, and your life will not have the fullness and abundance that the scripture says that you can have.

Moving out of the realm of depression

You cannot move out of something unless you know that you are there. That's like telling someone to move out of the aisle, but if they did not know, that they were in the aisle, they would probably stay right there. Depression is a funny illness. I call it an illness, because it carries with it all the symptomatic expressions, of a natural cold. You become fatigued, uninspired about life activities, and your production diminishes, as well as a host of other detrimental behaviors that outwardly manifest. But let me share something with you. I lived in a depressed state for a long time and fight the tendency even now to not let it be the thorn that overtakes me. But I figured out that depression is activated when an individual is not being their fully realized self (their true authentic self).

First, some of us live in depression every day, and we refuse to acknowledge that something is wrong. You must move out of the realm of depression, or you will run the risk of never looking within yourself, and becoming the real you.

We often forfeit our true identities for a false image of something or someone else. God has made us all to do a certain specific thing, but the hardest part is identifying what that thing is and then stepping over fear to accomplish what our purpose is. Fear, disappointment, and a pattern of rejection has crippled our imaginations and made us believe that God has forgotten about us, when the real issue lies in the fact that we have forgotten about him working in us. People all over the world are searching for themselves.

Instead of searching for that "self" that lies beyond the veil of smiles and grins, they turn towards fatalistic thinking.

Every person who has not been authentic to self will see that fatalistic thinking person inside. They will always think the absolute worse about everything. Fatalistic people are also those who constantly battle with completing things that they start. They don't have legitimate reasons for stopping, but they somehow cannot start the project again. These people battle with high negativity and low self-image. They will forfeit their dreams for another person's dream or vision, or simply talk themselves out of it, with their continual cycle of high negativity. When faced with adversity, they immediately confer with the negative side of life and contend that maybe that is how life is supposed to be for them. They are extreme negativists. Once they start talking negative, they can't stop. It's almost like a self-induced drug. Soon after they have exalted all the negativity in their life, their energy level dwindles to almost nothing, opening the door for depression.

If only they could see the worth of their negative situation from God's word. Solomon, the wisest man in the world, said it so rightly, *As a man thinks in his heart, so is he*. So it is the mind of a person that must be renewed, in order for the healing of past wounds to occur. People have become sick in their bodies because of how they allow their minds to think negative of the situation. As Isaiah says, "…there is no soundness in them, only wounds, bruises and putrefying sores, which have not been closed, mollified, or bound up" (Isaiah 1:6-7).

So, I thoroughly encourage you to look "within yourself" and find the real you, as I had to and I am so glad that I did. Although my process began more than 18 years ago, I know the struggle of just living out the true me every day. I realize that I had to hit "reset on my mindset" so that I could experience true freedom in Christ and let it spill over into other areas of my life. But now I am on the other side. I am acquainted with the beauty of being the real me. There is absolutely nothing more refreshing than to see God's light fully shine through me, without the desire to please anyone but Him. You will be made whole, and God shall get the glory out of your life.

Continue to do the following:

- Be true where you are.

- Never trust the option of failure.

- Give yourself room to grow.

- Allow yourself the time needed to make the transitions.

- Get an accountability partner who will love you through the process but hold you to your deliverance.

- Set up times for your soul to have an encounter with God, and never give into the lies that the enemy and you will speak over your life.

- Hold true to that which is good, and perfect (God's word), and apply it to your life.

These are simple things but can seem so difficult when you are right in the middle of the battle of your mind. You will win but knowing the "how" of the "what" is going to help you remain focused on your "why."

We are overcomers, so let's act like it together!

As you can probably tell, I could go on and on about the ups and downs of finding myself within. However, I would like for the last portion of my story to reflect what I now know.

What I Now Know

We are all scarred by life's perpetual ups and downs. The ups and downs are characterized by our disappointments, rejections, and failures. Some of which is not or has been the choosing of our own. When we look outside of ourselves, sometimes we only see what we have mirrored all our life, and this image cripples us from being the women we are destined to be.

At times, to think about being healed from past hurts and disappointment was too overwhelming, and thus I relinquished my quest to become whole. I soon found out that to exert any effort of being whole or complete is exemplary and should be commended, I know that for all those times I sat trying to understand and grapple with the pain of my childhood, all the frustration, anguish, craziness, and emptiness did nothing for me but cause me to sink deeper into depression.

I know now that when life tries to make me feel less than I am, I don't have to give into the pressures of not eating (becoming anorexic), sleeping all day or not at all, or being overly sexually active. I don't have to succumb to any of these things, and you don't either, because God is our friend who will stick closer than any brother, and He loves us very much. Know that healing is an element that provides the door for wholeness, and completeness to take place. As you continue to allow God to shape you and mold you into the model he wants, just be patient with yourself. You will outlast the others. In Christ this is a guarantee.

CHAPTER REFLECTION:

1. How has this chapter touched your life?

2. How can you share your experience to empower
    someone else?

3. When will you share your experience?

Write your responses to the above reflection in the *Woman of Purpose, Power and Passion Companion Journal*, to remind you of your personal commitment to yourself, and your passion to empower other women and young girls worldwide.

Sherae Bell

Sherae Bell is a licensed minister, and founder of *God Notes Ministries.* She is also a co-founder of *Cut for Christ Ministries.* She is an inspirational speaker with hopes to touch everyone's life that she comes across with a humble spirit. It is her desire to help others discover the full call of God on their lives. Born and raised in Baltimore City, MD to the late James and Lula Boller on October 13, 1964, the youngest of seven children. Sherae is an advocate for finding a cure for cancer, which has motivated her to participate in fundraisers since 2008 in hopes of finding a cure.

Her passion is to see women delivered and set free from the captivity of their past through her inspirational passages and the true word of God. Her motto is "from a past of shame to a future of deliverance." Sherae has been blessed to have lived in several states throughout the USA. North Carolina was her favorite, and California was her desert experience. California was where her spiritual walk became more intimate, and she began to know who she was called to be in Christ. Sherae has desired to write for years, but she had no clue what she would write about. Through God's faithfulness, Sherae now knows that He has ordained her past as her platform for her ministry; "transparency" is her life's word. Currently, Sherae resides in Leesburg, VA with her husband of 23 years Elder James Bell, and daughter Jazmyn Bell, 22.

Sherae is the proud mother of a son, Antonio Boller, 27, residing in Columbia, SC with his wife Jillisa-Nicole and children Anashija, 8, D'Amonte, 7, and Kaiden, 1. She is truly blessed!

Speaking Engagements & Special Event Contact Information:

Sherae Bell

704 Somerset Park Dr. SE #303

Leesburg, VA 20175

PH: 703-728-0036

Email: sherae64@yahoo.com

CHAPTER SEVEN

There is Purpose in Your Past

---

*"When God has a purpose, a plan, and
destiny for your life; nothing will and
can stop it from coming to fruition."*
—*Sherae Bell*

Lord, I usher in the presence of the Holy Spirit and ask you
to take full control of my every word, my every thought, and
my every emotion as I fulfill the purpose of your calling and
destiny on my life. I ask you to reveal to each reader your
purpose and plan for their future, no matter what it looks like
at this point and time. Help all of us to understand that our
time is no match for your time, but if we seek you, our timing
will coincide with your time and all things desired, ordained,
and destined will come to pass. Remind us that you are the
author and finisher of our peace, and you hold the key to our
future. It was you who created us and know us better than
we know ourselves. Lord, I ask you to open our ears to hear,
our eyes to see, and our hearts to understand your call on our
life. In Jesus's name, we receive it and believe it and call it
all as done. Amen!

As I was thinking of situations where God has shown himself true to me, he brought to my mind the road I travelled to get to this season.

Ecclesiastes 3:1, *"There is a time for everything, and a season for every activity under the heavens."* (NIV)

God has already ordained our destinies, but we are not always in tune with him to realize that we have the victory over any trials or tribulations that come against us. Walking with the Lord is such a great but challenging experience that can only bring out the best in anyone who seeks Him wholeheartedly without any reservations. Thinking back over my life, I see so many times when the Lord was with me, teaching me and preparing me for greater things, without me knowing.

I allowed the devil to use fear, insecurity, shame, and unworthiness to determine what my future was going to be by buying into every scheme, every vain imagination, and every lie. I later learned the devil was the father of lies, and I easily allowed him to overtake me.

John 8:44, *"You belong to your father, the devil, and you want to carry out your father's desires. He was a murderer from the beginning, not holding to the truth, for there is no truth in him. When he lies, he speaks his native language, for he is a liar and the father of lies."* (NIV)

I gave him a place in my life where I knew he had no authority to reside.

In Ephesians 4:26-27 it says, "*Be ye angry, and sin not: let not the sun go down upon your wrath: Neither give place to the devil.*" (NIV) I had already begun it to give him.

The Lord was continuously bringing people into my life to speak a word of deliverance, freedom, and destiny. I felt that my past was a much greater deterrent than whatever goodness would be in my future. In other words, I was naïve to the power of God and had no clue to what it meant for God to have purpose for me.

In Proverbs 19:21 it says that "*Many plans are in a man's mind, but it is the Lord's purpose for him that will stand.*" (NIV)

Therefore, no matter what I thought was my purpose or my future God's plan was still going to prevail. Even though there were seasons in my life of sexual immorality, thievery, gossiping, and backbiting.

Romans 3:23, "*For everyone has sinned; we all fall short of God's glorious standard.*" (NLV)

However, God continued to bless me no matter my state of commitment to Him. I was not committed to giving Him my all, nor did I want to give up what I was familiar with to tread on waters that I was unfamiliar with. I knew the temperature and the deepness of the waters that I was in and what it offered; therefore, my commitment was to the familiar. However, I was very unsure and fearful of what the untested waters of my future entailed, that I was not willing to allow myself to explore it in this season of my life.

Proverbs 28:13, *"People who conceal their sins will not prosper, but if they confess and turn from them, they will receive mercy."* (NIV)

I did not realize, nor did I understand that all the things I had encountered were a set-up for all the things that God had already ordained for me if I chose the unfamiliar waters.

Romans 8:28, *"And we know that in all things God works for the good of those who love him, who have been called according to his purpose."* (NIV)

So that brings me to the point of where I thought I was at my lowest. Can you say, "jail time"? Yes, I spent time behind the steel bars for something that seemed so trivial to me at the time, but it would be a self-discovering period and life-altering lesson for things to come in my future. It was at that point that the three characteristics of the devil tried to take hold of my life. But who knows that God always has a plan? The thief known as the devil had come to kill, steal and destroy me in any way possible because even he knew that God had a plan.

John 10:10, *"The thief cometh not, but for to steal, and to kill, and to destroy: I am come that they might have life, and that they might have it more abundantly."* (NIV)

I was caught shoplifting, convicted and sentenced to forty-eight hours in jail. I used term forty-eight hours instead of two days so you could understand the agony that would soon be my short-term destiny. Not a long time, but enough time for God to get His point across and for me to know this was neither my, nor my newborn son's destiny.

When you start out shoplifting, it begins sometimes as a child just taking gum, candy bars, and anything at the checkout counter that may be in your hand's reach. Some people may consider it to be somewhat cute when you are a child, and the grown-ups say, "Oh, he or she is just a child. They don't know what they are doing; they will grow out of it."

But as that child grows and realizes that they need to start hiding the evidence and only eating or using it when they are by themselves, it is no longer cute. That child is now displaying acts of knowledge between what is right and what is wrong. In that case if the adult in that situation still thinks it is cute, we need to check that adult. But of course, this was not my situation because if my parents had known I would have been in for a rude awakening.

The word of God's says in Proverbs 22:6, *"Train up a child in the way he should go; even when he is old he will not depart from it."* (NIV)

And maybe if they had known I would not have been wearing my new designer clothes walking down the runway of the jail corridor. So from gum, candy bars and small items on to other things that I thought would fill a void in me and heal my brokenness. But you say how could there be brokenness in a child?

Something had to be broken in any child or me whose parents gave them all that they needed and most of what they desired to travel down this road. Nothing that my parents had done brought me to this point. My dad sang in a gospel group, and we went to church. For the most part, I knew of the Lord; well, I should say that I knew that there was someone greater than man himself, but I didn't know how great. I believe that what we do as children, if never brought to the light and if not countered by something positive will move us into a destiny of brokenness as we become adults.

Psalm 147:3, *"He heals the brokenhearted and binds up their wounds."* (NIV)

So you say, "But how could I be broken?" I just had this handsome baby boy to share my life with and to call my own.

Psalm 127:3, *"Behold, children are a heritage from the Lord, the fruit of the womb a reward."* (KJV)

Someone who I would love unconditionally, no holds barred, because he was mine. He would know no more about me than what I would tell him which would only be the good things. He was a part of me that no one could ever take from me and he would love me unconditionally. I would have a part in creating his destiny. But, there still seemed to still be something missing. I needed someone that I did not have to groom into loving me unconditionally, but someone that would accept me with all my faults and my shameful past.

But instead, I continued to hide who I really was behind the clothes I wore, the lifestyle I tried to live, and the company that I tried to keep. I had what I called an inner circle. But how could they be my inner circle if they really did not know me at all? All they knew was this alter ego that I had created, who appeared to be strong and very sure of herself. No one could ever know that I was struggling with my life and that I was scared to death to raise my son alone. This is not how my life was supposed to be. I lived it in the manner I felt was appealing to the people in my circle and in the way I thought that it should have been.

My life was full of potential, but it just was not happening as fast as I thought that it should. I had been in the Army Reserves for 4 years, experienced some college, and I had a good job working at the hospital, which I lost because of missing work when I was in jail. I know that you are probably saying, "but it was only 2 days." That should not have been that hard to do. Same thing I said and thought. Yes, I had a job, but that money was to take care of my son and not to fill my void or to fix my brokenness. I wasn't realizing that getting caught could possibly release me from taking care of my son forever; it could all come to an end because of my desires and my lack of judgment. I needed to keep up this great farce of being more than I was and someone that I was not.

So here I am trying to keep up with the "Joneses;" by the way, who in the world are the "Joneses"? I didn't know them personally, but their name was so popular that they had to be some very important people and people that anybody would want to be just like. Well anyway, I was in K-Mart, and I saw the cutest outfit that I just had to have. Yes, K-Mart that was the place to shop and if there are still any in your area, K-Mart can still be the place to shop. I had done it before so what would make shoplifting at K-Mart this time any different from any other time? Well, what made this time different is that I got caught. I pleaded to the security and with the store manager that if they let me go, I would never steal again and never come back into K-Mart again. But that did not work because they both said they heard that before by others and they would not be doing their jobs if they did not report it, nor would they be helping me. I could not see how they were helping me by reporting it, but the lesson was still to be learned.

The police gave me notice to appear in court for the judge to decide. I did not tell my family and I denied to my nephew that it was true. Then the day came for me to appear in court and I went by myself, and I pleaded guilty. Yes, I pleaded guilty because I was not in denial about what I had done. I knew that it was wrong, but I also thought the outcome would be different. I thought the judge was going to let me go because to his knowledge I had never stolen before. But he was one of those judges that thought if he had not shown me right from wrong, I would be back in the same situation again. So he sentenced me to two days in the county jail. I thought to myself for a moment, only two days, what was that going to do, how could any lessons be taught and learned in such a short time? Those were my sentiments. But when I heard "two days, forty-eight hours" it was like I heard him say "life" in prison. My heart sank and my tears began to flow. Now I had to face the reality of being exposed of one of my deepest darkest secrets. I was a thief and considered a convict by all definitions of the word.

The deputy clerk processed my paperwork, and I was escorted to my jail cell! I was immediately stripped of my clothes, given an orange jumper and white sneakers, stripped of my identity, given a number, stripped of my pride and forced to into a humbling position of search and seizure. Then to make matters even worse, I was thrown into a courtyard with many others who had also been stripped of their identity. When I got a chance, I called my sister crying and asked her to get my son from the baby-sitter because I was in jail. All I could think about was never seeing my son again, the little person that was so much a part of me that he was even with me when I committed the crime. Well, he was always with me, that day was supposed to be no different than any other day. He was mine, my little sidekick, what I considered to be everything to me.

Please do not judge me--I have done enough of that for myself. No judgment allowed, only healing and deliverance. I apologized to my family for not telling them and trying to handle it on my own. What's done in the dark will be brought to the light. Again, when the sentence came down my thoughts were how could me spending forty-eight hours in jail teach me any lessons or serve any purpose? It was just forty-eight hours. But you see when God has a purpose, a plan and destiny for your life; nothing will and can stop it from coming to fruition. It does not take Him a lifetime to get His point across. This was a time that I would begin to build my trust and grow in the Lord. This was the beginning of my lesson to not let pride take up residence in my life and not be concerned about what others saw or thought of me. It brought to the forefront of my mind and opened my heart even more to understand the strong love and the bond that I had for my son and that I needed to be there to provide for his every need accordingly.

It gave me time to get myself together so that I would never travel down that road again, and most importantly, it was enough time for God to show me that He still loved me, had not forgotten about me. He was still watching over me in the mist of my mess.

Hebrews 13:5, "*Keep your lives free from the love of money and be content with what you have, because God has said, 'Never will I leave you; never will I forsake you.'*" (NIV)

So you wonder whatever happened to that beautiful baby boy that I cherished so much. Well, he is now 27 years old with a family of his own. God is so good. I have never stolen since that day. Do I still struggle with life's challenges? Of course I do, but now I know who holds the keys to my future. Oh, what an awesome God we serve! He loved me even when I didn't want to love myself and when I wanted to be loved so much by people that could not guarantee my life nor were they a part of His plan for my future. They had no clue as to what God had done, was doing, and was going to do.

1st Corinthians 2:9, "*However, as it is written: 'What no eye has seen, what no ear has heard, and what no human mind has conceived' the things God has prepared for those who love him, these are the things God has revealed to us by his Spirit.'*" (NIV)

God was doing a work in me, and it was for such a time as this during my time of trials and tribulations to bring forth His glory. He prepares us in ways unbeknownst to us that will serve the purpose for Him. God watched over me and

He had already ordered my steps even when I tried to choose the path that seemed to be the most travelled by others.

Proverbs 16:9, *"In their hearts humans plan their course, but the LORD establishes their steps."* (NIV)

I was not built for that path for, nor was I designed to handle it, for it was a road of destruction. I often ask myself during that time in my life did I really believe that I had hope traveling in the territory that I truly was not familiar with? Why wouldn't I trust myself to the one who had created me?

The word of God says in Jeremiah 29:11, *"For I know the plans I have for you, declares the LORD, plans to prosper you and not to harm you, plans to give you hope and a future."* (NIV)

The power of God reigns forever, and His glory cannot and will not be denied. You see God had to take me to what I thought was the lowest point in my life, where I couldn't face myself. I didn't even want to be acquainted with myself, but for me to begin to see the person that He was creating me to be, I had to lay down everything that was keeping me from moving forward in Him.

Hebrews 12:1, *"Therefore, since we are surrounded by such a great cloud of witnesses, let us throw off everything that hinders and the sin that so easily entangles, and let us run with perseverance the race marked out for us."* (NIV)

His creation is still being molded in me to this day. To be that woman that knows she has a destiny, a woman that possesses passion, a woman who embraces her power, a woman that seeks out her purpose, a woman that trusts that she has promise, and most of all a woman that really knows her worth. As a woman I realized I must always to keep the following things close to me:

My **destiny** was set for me from the day I was formed in my mother's womb, an inhabitant of GOD's greatness that is determined by HIS standard and for HIS glory.

Jeremiah 1:5, *"Before I formed you in the womb I knew you, before you were born I set you apart."* (NIV)

My **passion** has been established to please God in every aspect of my life, no matter what it takes it has already been placed in my spirit, my acceptance has already been granted.

Colossians 3:23-24, *"Whatever you do, work at it with all your heart, as working for the Lord, not for human masters, since you know that you will receive an inheritance from the Lord as a reward."* (NIV)

My **power** is given to me by God as a believer in Him through grace to rebuke the enemy and know that he will fly.

Luke 10:19, "*I have given you authority to trample on snakes and scorpions and to overcome all the power of the enemy; nothing will harm you.*" (NIV)

My **purpose** in life is to reach a level of holiness that seems to be unattainable to the natural eye, but so real to me.

Philippians 3:14, "*I press toward the mark for the prize of the high calling of God in Christ Jesus.*" (KJV)

My **promise** is to be committed to the things of God and to His word to lead me to the road of righteousness.

Psalm 32:8, "*I will instruct you and teach you in the way you should go; I will counsel you with my loving eye on you.*" (NIV)

My **worth** is more valuable than any other creation on earth and so intricately made that there is no substitute for me.

Isaiah 64:8, "*But now, O LORD, thou art our father; we are the clay, and thou our potter; and we all are the work of thy hand.*" (KJV)

Since I did not know that my destiny had already been set for my life I was heading down a road that had me thinking that I was lacking something or needed something greater materialistically.

Proverbs 29:18, *"Where there is no revelation, people cast off restraint; but blessed is the one who heeds wisdom's instruction."* (NIV)

But that was only by the limitations that I had placed on myself trying to live up to man's standards.

God's word says in Philippians 4:13, *"I can do all things through Christ who strengthens me."* (NIV)

This means that there is no limit to the ability that God has placed in me. I had put myself in a place where I could be judged by the lack of or the value of the material things that I possessed because I had no faith in knowing the real substance of my being which God had placed in me.

Psalm 139:14, *"I praise you because I am fearfully and wonderfully made; your works are wonderful, I know that full well."*

Only God could place a value on my worth and He said that I was just what He needed for the plan He was establishing to go forth with His word. God loves me unconditionally and there will be times when I slip and stumble but if I put my trust in Him, I will never fall into a hole that is too deep that it will consume me. He reminded me that He could use my every mistake, shortcoming, and trial for His glory. I now know that I am never too far that God cannot reach me.

Psalm 139:8, *"If I ascend up into heaven, thou art there: if I make my bed in hell, behold, thou art there."* (KJV)

God has allowed my past to be used as my platform for my ministry to glorify Him. I have always heard the saying, "God is doing a new thing," but if God's word says in Ecclesiastes 1:9 that, *"What has been will be again, what has been done will be done again; there is nothing new under the sun."* (NIV) He is doing the same thing. God is just beginning to trust me more with the unfolding and revelation of the things that He has already ordained in me. This is a clear attribute of God which is His immutability to not change as it says in Hebrews 13:8 that, *"Jesus Christ is the same yesterday and today and forever."* (NIV)

We have to come to the knowledge and understanding of God in our lives and who we are in Him before He can reveal some things to us.

2 Peter 3:18, *"But grow in the grace and knowledge of our Lord and Savior Jesus Christ. To him is glory both now and forever! Amen."* (NIV)

So until we come to the full understanding that nothing happens without purpose we will not be able to completely comprehend and live a life of holiness and be dedicated to the cause of Jesus Christ.

1 Peter 1:15, *"But as the one who called you is holy, you yourselves also be holy in all your conduct and manner of living."* (NIV)

Jesus died so that we could be free from bondage and live a life of abundance through Him. We are no longer bound by the chains of sin and the law that leads us down a path of death, but the word of God says in Matthew 6:33, *"But seek ye first the kingdom of God, and his righteousness; and all these things shall be added unto you."* (KJV)

In conclusion, I ask you to hold onto God's unchanging hand and know that He wants the best for you.

Psalm 84:11, *"For the LORD God is a sun and shield; the LORD bestows favor and honor; no good thing does he withhold from those whose walk is blameless."* (NIV)

He never puts more on us then we can bear always providing a way of escape to remain faithful to Him as He is to us.

1st Cor. 10:13, *"There hath no temptation taken you but such as is common to man: but God is faithful, who will not suffer you to be tempted above that ye are able; but will with the temptation also make a way to escape, that ye may be able to bear it."* (KJV)

The Lord will provide our every need and will not leave us to suffer.

147

Philippians 4:19, *"And my God will meet all your needs according to the riches of his glory in Christ Jesus."* (NIV)

I ask you to take time to seek God for His direction in your life, believe and trust in HIS word and know that HE will not lead you astray.

Hebrews 11:6, *"But without faith it is impossible to please Him. For He that cometh to God must believe that He is, and that He is a Rewarder of those who diligently seek Him."* (KJV)

There is purpose for your life, purpose in your life and purpose in the path that you have walked thus far. Give it all to Him, withholding no small thing from Him and allow Him to use every tear, every hurt and every disappointment for His glory.

Deuteronomy 30:6, *"The LORD your God will circumcise your hearts and the hearts of your descendants, so that you may love him with all your heart and with all your soul, and live."* (NIV)

Know that He loves you and that He wants you to love Him with everything that is within you.

Matthew 22:37-38, *"Jesus replied: 'Love the Lord your God with all your heart and with all your soul and with all your mind. This is the first and greatest commandment."* (NIV)

Lord, thank you for this great opportunity that you have afforded me to share one of my life's seasons. I pray that it has set someone free from their state of captivity and their past of shame. I pray that they have come to understand our journey is not always for us but for others to see the glory of God through us. I thank you for this season; it has helped me to be who you have called me to be. Continue to show yourself true and let your glory reign forever in us. Touch each person that has read this and place an awesome anointing on their life, give them that great power that you encompass and the passion you have for their freedom in you.

Show the reader how to forgive themselves of their past transgressions and how to move forward in your grace and the knowledge of your son Jesus Christ. Lord birth the gift you have placed in them and give them what they need to accomplish all that's predestined for them and establish that which your word confirms in Philippians 1:6, *"Being confident of this, that he who began a good work in you will carry it on to completion until the day of Christ Jesus."* Give them a peace about their past and a voice for their future.

I speak Romans 4:17 over their life for it says, *"As it is written, I have made you a father of many nations in the presence of him whom he believed-God, who gives life to the dead, and calls those things which do not exist as though they did."*

149

So I ask you to give life to that which seems to be dead. Lord I ask you to grant to them the desires of their heart but remind them of your word in Matthew 6:33, *"But seek first his kingdom and his righteousness, and all these things will be given to you as well."*

Giving them understanding that sometimes denial may just be a delay. Finally Lord, we thank you for every form of correction that will catapult us into our destiny and we thank you in advance in the mighty name of Jesus. Amen!

CHAPTER REFLECTION:

1. What is holding you hostage from experiencing the fullness of God?

2. Has God been tugging at your heart about HIS plan for your life?

3. What are some of the trials that can be used to set your path straight?

Write your responses to the above reflection in the *Woman of Purpose, Power and Passion Companion Journal*; and pray that God uses your life as a testimony as to His power, for His glory and His honor.

The last chapter of *Woman of Purpose, Power and Passion* will help you to maximize your purpose in life even more! You may need another *Woman of Purpose, Power and Passion Companion Journal*, before you start. Get another copy at, bit.ly/wop-2014-journal.

To get published in the next anthology sign up at, bit.ly/wop-registration.

Laura Bella

Laura Bella is the founder and the CEO of Laura Bella International. LBI is an organization dedicated to enriching and empowering the lives of young women all over the World. A Lifestyle coach, inspirational speaker, author, model, and vocalist, crowned Ms. Plus America 2006-2007, she is also the winner of six international awards in modeling, singing, and acting. Laura is grateful for the international sales of her Empowering Affirmation and Leadership CD's. She is also a co-author of the *Woman of Purpose, Power, and Passion* Anthology.

Laura has achieved a bronze level executive director position, with Pre-Paid Legal Services, Inc., a company devoted to creating equal justice for everyone. She also enjoys being an active volunteer in her community and throughout the world with various organizations including PSI World.

Speaking Engagement & Special Event Contact
Information:

Laura Bella
P.O. Box 90931
LA, CA 90009
PH: 424-225-1152
Email: laurabella26@gmail.com

CHAPTER EIGHT

Keys to Living and Loving Yourself and Your Blissful Life

"I am a divine creation, I am a vessel of unconditional love, worthy of giving and receiving love abundantly."
—*Laura Bella*

First Key: Self-Love

What is your legacy? Has anyone ever asked you want you want yours to be or are you already living it? It's so easy to get caught up in a busy life of doing this and that, going through the motions of life not often remembering why you're here. In my own journey of self-discovery, I've realized that everything leading up to this moment has been part of my divine path.

Now, I'm more conscious of the life I'm leading, the lessons I learn/teach, the example I set by simple acts of kindness in every moment. Instead of doing I focus on being. That may seem like a foreign concept for you however, keep reading and you'll catch what I'm talking about. Perhaps this isn't new information for you; however, I wanted to be a part of this special book so that I could share some of the valuable lessons I've learned from my life experiences as well as from my amazing coaches, mentors, teachers, books, seminars, etc. I will share some exercises, stories, and affirmations that will guide you on a positive, loving path towards your purpose and leaving the legacy you desire.

I am a divine creation, I am a vessel of unconditional love, worthy of giving and receiving love abundantly. The area of love covers so much and is the foundation of my existence and it has been quite a journey over the last several years to come to this place. Realizing your self-worth can be a lot more challenging than it seems. I have personally invested over $100,000 in my own personal development to fall completely in love with the person I am and what I see in the mirror, and the woman I'm becoming in every moment. Are you able to look at yourself naked in the mirror and say that you love and accept every part of yourself?

Here's an exercise to determine where you are:

What do you see when you look in the mirror? Name three things you love about your face, your body, and your personality? What makes you beautiful? If you aren't able to see three things at first, don't worry, we've all been there. I can relate to not loving what's in the mirror, heck, I'm a work in progress. Although I do love my *curvalicious* body, I'm heavier than I've been in a few years. Because I do love myself and want to be the healthiest version of myself, I'm currently working with a training coach so that I can fall in love with all my beautiful curves again and become even healthier.

Even though I don't have the figure I know I'm meant to have, I give myself love as if I do. When I'm in the shower, I talk to myself and love my body like this: *"I am so happy and grateful for my sexy, healthy, toned, cellulite-free, beautiful legs. I am so happy and grateful for my beautiful, full, healthy, soft hair."* Does this seem crazy to you? Well, let me tell you I'm a huge believer in positive affirmations and the power that words have and how you speak them to yourself. Most of the great personal development books/speakers teach this; act as if until you have it. Your language and your inner self work are so powerful, they truly dictate every part of your life, so speak your powerful self and believe your words. Another way to recognize my own self-love is reflected around me from others, as they reflect me.

If you've been on an airplane, you've probably noticed the safety announcement whereby they instruct you to put on your oxygen mask and then assist your children/loved ones. Ever wonder why? Well, you must make sure you're taken care of first before you can help others. That being said you are number one. Make sure you take time to take care of your needs and then taking care of others will probably be that much easier. On the flip side, if you're needs are not met, how can you take care of anyone else? There's a saying, "give from the overflow." This to me means that as long as I'm putting myself first, serving/helping/supporting others from the overflow is nearly effortless. Let me tell you it took a lot of time to realize how important this is and we'll talk more about this in the coming pages.

Boundaries are still an area that I continue to work on, as these are an important part of loving yourself. I used to allow myself to be imposed upon because of a poor self-image, fear of conflict, and uncertainty about my right to exercise control over my life. Once the self-love was realized and truly part of my core, I began to take a stand for myself and let others know how I expected to be treated. Know when it's time to say no. If something doesn't feel right, listen to that, take a moment and make a conscious decision. Decide that you value yourself enough to draw these lines and value others enough to teach them how to be with you.

Boundaries are critical to loving yourself and creating the life that works for you. Journal your feelings on boundaries for 10 minutes. Are you happy with these boundaries? If yes, then write how they can be even better? If no, why not and how can you open the communication with the receiver to create the best win-win relationship?

Second Key: Spirituality

I am a divine creation, I embrace this perfect day with joy, bliss, and everything I intend to move forward towards my greatest good.

When you awake in the morning, before you get out of bed, what is the first thing you think about, the first thing you do? Do you start the day grumpy, or do you embrace the day as a fresh start with a smile on your face? Do you pray? Do you meditate? When I awake, I set my intention for the day, what I hope to accomplish and with the attitude I intend to be. If meditating seems like too much for you right now, then at least start with this exercise. Before you leap out of bed and jump-start into your busy day, stop and take a few deep breaths, visualize the incredible day you're going to have, and state a few things you're grateful for. At the end of the day, notice how your days change now that you've begun them this way and journal 10+ minutes/day on how you feel now.

Another part of spirituality is envisioning. Have you ever thought about an outcome you wanted for a project or goal you were working on? Did you take time to really envision the desired outcome? If so, did it turn out the way you hoped?

Was your result what you wanted? Sometimes, things don't look exactly as we imagine; however, the end result is often greater than we ever dreamed of. Let me share a great story with you about visioning and affirmations (as these go hand in hand).

A few years ago, I was selected as *Ms. Plus Illinois* (my hometown state), with just a few weeks before the National competition; we were instructed to bring a gift from our hometown for the reigning Queens and state delegates. Well, I decided to go in the studio and record my first Affirmation CD.

I had been coached/mentored with similar tools and knew how powerful they are. Minutes before I went into the studio, my coach was working with me to perfect the language for this project and was behind me 100% and I was so excited (I love being in the studio). I created my first Affirmation CD as a gift and then had the producer create a separate one for me whereby one of the lines was, "I am *Ms. Plus America* 2006." For the next three weeks, I heard this and it continued to sink into my subconscious. As I visualized myself donning the formal wear of the national's competition and gliding the stage as if the crown was already on my head. My mind heard that I was the Queen and I already believed it, the next step was simply to take the action.

Minutes later they announce that I'm in the Top 5, then it's down to myself and *Ms. California* as the final two. We're standing there, waiting for them to announce the winner and then it's said, "The new *Ms. Plus America* is Laura Bella." I nearly lost it and my mom later said she about fell out of her chair. I have to share that up until this moment, I never had the confidence to model, nor had I ever participated in a pageant of any kind. This may seem like a miracle to many; however, the power of suggestion and how we speak to our subconscious/conscious mind is so powerful. I imagine there is something phenomenal that has happened in your life from your visioning, and I look forward to hearing about it.

A fun exercise for you:

Get together a bunch of friends and have them bring over magazines and create vision/dream boards for the life you want. Keep the dream board visible and look at it every day as a reminder to the life/lifestyle you want; you may be surprised as to how quickly things can come about from this. Go to iTunes or my site and download my Affirmation Cd's and please let me know how things begin to change/transform in your life.

Third Key: Support

I am a divine creation; I love and accept support into my life in all forms and for this I am so grateful. If you look back on your life, chances are that there were people supporting you to get you through specific times/goals in your life. If you were part of a team than you had a coach and team members that held you accountable of being/doing your best. If you were never part of a team, then perhaps think back on how your mom/dad was/is your biggest fan/cheerleader.

One of the biggest challenges for me, I must admit, has been reaching out and asking for support. I was quite independent growing up and did many things on my own, sound familiar at all? To this day, I must remind myself that I know better and things with support are so much easier and most of the times your friends/loved ones are happy to help especially because there will probably come a time when they'll need your support, too.

You don't have to do it alone; we were meant to be in partnership with one another. Just recently I experienced a great loss in my life like nothing I've ever gone through, and it's a challenge still every day to think about it and not tear up or simply cry. However, one of the many blessings that came from this loss was realizing all the love and support around me. It is invaluable to me how much my friends and family stepped up to listen, hug, and console me. Without them I could not have gotten through it, and for this I am so grateful and thankful for the support in my life.

Part of self-love is realizing your self-worth and investing in yourself to reach out for coaches and mentors. There are so many invaluable things that can be gained from support like: learning how to create solutions when facing a challenge and having accountability to reach a goal. I've been fortunate to have a few key people in my life that have seen me greater than I've seen myself; they saw my ultimate potential, success, beauty in times where I couldn't see it for myself.

Sound familiar in your life? Creating a support team is a critical part to loving yourself and living the life of bliss that you deserve. Another aspect of success in my life has been acquiring specific coaches that can guide me from point A to point B. Most of the great leaders of our time and before us have always had coaches to support their goals and continue to be routinely coached. Coaches can give you the tools to uncover your purpose, your gifts and ultimately allow you to fall in love with who you are. A vital part of being coached is being open to the possibility of internal growth; it's important to listen and be present. Another great part of support is accountability. I am so grateful because a few years ago I went through a 90-day goal setting program that later became vital to loving myself and continuing to build my blissful life. Not only did I have the team to support me, I also had an amazing coach. During my reign as *Ms. Plus America*, I was selected to compete on the US team for the *World Championship of Performing Arts* amongst 70 countries in the areas of modeling, acting, and singing.

I thought *Ms. Plus America* was big, but this was beyond anything I imagined. In preparation for the competition, we trained for several months, as it's like the Olympics for performing arts. I had some huge goals to obtain before competing on such a large stage and my coach and team held me accountable to reaching these goals. I competed in nine competitions and took home six medals. Are you kidding me? The proudest moment for me was winning a gold medal in plus modeling for swimwear. Remember that I am that girl that grew up insecure and chubby my whole life hearing things like, *"Laura is so pretty, if only she lost weight."* Well, sometimes kids don't say the nicest things and it has a way of sticking until the days finally come where you've done enough work on yourself to realize you love your perfect imperfect self no matter what anyone else says and now, I had the gold medals to prove how beautiful and talented I am.

Exercise: Think about the support in your life. Does it look the way you want it to? Could there be things you could ask for support in as an exchange with a friend/colleague? How could this change/improve your life for the better? Do you have big goals that you'd like to be held accountable for? If so, then perhaps it's time to consider a coach. Feel free to reach out to me for support on this.

Fourth Key: Relationships

I love and appreciate the beautiful relationships I create in my life.

I am not going to pretend that this is a section that I am yet completely comfortable with (however, I am working on it daily). A few years ago, I was honored to have a millionaire coach me to take my business and my life to the next level.

During one of our sessions the topic of my relationships came up whereby he stated to me, *"Laura, you have the relationships in your life because this is how you created them, why do you push people away?"* Wow! He's right. Up until that moment I didn't quite get it, and I then realized that I am the common denominator in the relationships I've created. What I also realized was the main reason why I pushed people away or kept them at a distance was because from a young age, the people closest to me left. How could I allow anyone to get close to my heart if they were going to leave? Well, thankfully I later realized that connection is why we're here; it gives us purpose and meaning in our lives.

Even in writing this chapter, it is quite vulnerable for me to be discussing this because this is a place where I have struggled with most of my life. I also continue to work on the relationships with my family as well and fortunately we get closer each day. I am grateful to have amazing relationships across the world, however, it is my intention that I will continue to develop friendships in my local community--even if it means that they can or may walk away at any time.

Relationships are critical to living a blissful life, and the greatest relationship you can have is with yourself. After quite a bit of counseling and coaching, I realized that the people that left had little to do with me. People leaving is simply a part of life. Since I fall more and more in love with who I am each day, it's a gift to share more of who I am with others and to do my best not to hold back. This leads me to another important part of relationships, vulnerability and intimacy.

Let's talk about sex, baby... OK, so this is an interesting topic for many however, love and sex are the roots of most things/ideas/actions in life and being vulnerable has a lot to do with it.

One of my passions is dancing, so this is how I relate a lot of things. For me, dancing is a lot like relationships. For you, it could be something different, so feel free to relate this accordingly. Let's take ballroom dancing for example. To have a smooth, sexy, fun partner dance, the key is to surrender control to the lead. Let me tell you allowing the leader to lead is a challenging thing for me (and many years later it's still something that I sometimes struggle with). Of course, there are times when you want to lead in life and step into your dominant roll and that is completely OK. Everything has a balance, though. When you can allow your dominant side to lead you, it is a beautiful thing. In my last relationship, I remember a conversation whereby I stated to my sweetie something I wanted to support me in getting in shape and he says, *"Ok honey, there's a place near my house where I can get that for you."* Well, I quickly stepped in and said, *"I could probably find it on Amazon.com for less."* He immediately felt almost emasculated and frustrated replying, *"I was going to get it for you as a surprise, but if you want to get it yourself then feel free."* So I apologized and said something like, *"Honey, I apologize, I was so independent growing up, a go-getter, and I'm learning to allow the man in my life to be the man and I will work on it."*

Another great thing about dance for me is learning to trust my partner. This is a vital part of a relationship. If they don't feel like you can trust them, chances are they aren't going to open and share their heart and this could be a huge take for both of you.

EXERCISE: Go to someone you trust and ask them 3 things they find sexy about you. Then, listen and pay attention to how you feel when they say it. Are you able to truly receive this? Can you own these words they're sharing with you and do these qualities feel true for you? If not, then I invite you to spend one minute in the mirror every day, acknowledging your 3 sexy characteristics about yourself. If you can accept what they're saying than I challenge you to the same exercise; however, doing it naked in the mirror acknowledging yourself. This could feel uncomfortable in the beginning; however, eventually you'll probably love it.

Fifth Key: Health and Nutrition

As I love my body, I am so grateful for the healthy food I feed it and grow with.

Health and nutrition is an important element to loving yourself and there are many things to consider. Perhaps you're not able to relate because you've lived a healthy life, however, stay tuned as there is valuable information on how your relationship with food is so important to living a blissful life you love. About ten years ago, I was nearly 300 pounds and finally realized enough was enough. I was out of control, and if I continued this path, it was just a matter of time where I could find the fate of many diseases, so I decided to take positive action. I'm not going to sit here and tell you it was easy (and anyone who has struggled with weight may know what I'm talking about). It took a lot of work, many months, lots of support and changing my habits to conscious eating (I mean, let's be real, that much weight didn't come on over night and it was going to take time and effort to release it). For most of my life, food was my comfort; however, now that I was finally thinner, I wanted to maintain it and continue to get healthy. I started to pay attention to everything that goes into my body and notice how I feel as I'm eating. Am I full? Do I need to take another bite?

What I noticed was that as a heavy person I was living to eat and now I had to shift so that food served my body so that I'm simply eating to live. Another healthy habit I've obtained is to eat on smaller plates (usually 6-8 inches) that way I'm sure to not overeat and keep in mind of the portions of each type of food on your plate. I'm not a nutritionist; therefore, I recommend you speak with an expert about this. Portion control can be a challenge when eating out in many countries. However, whenever possible go for Tapas sized portions that you can share (this creates the social aspect and makes it fun). Another tip is to ask the waiter to box up half the meal before it's brought to the table, so you don't overindulge.

If all of this isn't working for you and you're still having issues with wanting more or self-control, I invite you to check in and listen to your body. What does it need? Why do you find yourself wanting more? Is there something you want to escape by continuing to eat?

Another important aspect to this area is to pay attention to what you are eating. By this I mean eating as healthy as possible. Reading labels and preparing your own healthy, non-GMO and preferably organic food is best so you know exactly what's going into your body; however, I recommend consulting with the experts in this arena so that they can customize a diet you love and enjoy. If you don't yet have the resources to hire an expert, then at least listen to your body, as it will often let you know what food it prefers.

Exercise: For the next thirty days I invite you to keep a food journal so that you can have some awareness around your relationship with food. Document what you eat and how you feel within 30-minutes after. How do you think or feel during the process? To make this fun, do this exercise with a buddy or a coach so you can share the journey together. Feel free to reach out to me and share your experiences, as I'd love to hear about them.

Sixth Key: Finding Your Joy in Movement

I love and accept my beautiful body as it flows and moves towards a healthier self.

As I mentioned, I grew up a chubby child and would get made fun of--can you relate? My mom put me in dance starting at age 8 and at the time, I didn't like it too much as I didn't look like the skinny girls in class, and my teacher was so disciplined (let's keep it real, she was mean). I continued to move from one style of dance to the other, hoping to find a place to fit in, but never really did. Finally, I realized it wasn't them, it was myself I wasn't accepting, I felt awkward. Of course, it didn't help any that not only was I chubby (and felt out of place), but all the other dancers were eating (what I considered to be) rabbit food as their snacks (while I ate junk food most of the time). I was like, *"I'm burning it off, right?"* These classes started an interesting perception of reality for me about society and what the American girl is supposed to look like.

This was at a time when being chubby, thick, or plus sized (as its most referred to) wasn't popular as it is now. Fortunately, I met a close friend in one of my dance classes and we hit it off quickly. We attended classes together and I was thrilled to finally feel like I fit in with someone. It makes such a difference to share the simple joys of life with other like-minded people that enjoy them as well. I started to come into my love of dance, and it became a large part of my life. I was the only *curvalicious* girl in *honors dance* during high school, and then went on to minor in dance at college. What's my point to all of this? Well, I love to dance, as it's a big part of how I exercise, stay healthy, express myself, and have fun, which is so important to ideal health and joy in life. For you though, it can be anything. What activities bring you joy? What brings out your sense of child-like fun? We were born for pleasure. Think about that young child that goes from pleasure activity to pleasure; there's got to be an activity out there that is fun for you. Exercise can be fun and enjoyable, and it's a great way to improve your health, stay fit, increase your stamina, and can also help with balance, poise, and how you carry yourself. Another option is to find an activity partner to join you so perhaps it is more enjoyable. If going to the gym or working out is not your cup of tea (and believe me I can relate), and then perhaps you could hire a coach/trainer to make it fun. Chances are they'll at least be nice to look at while you're busting your butt and they'll inspire you to keep going when you think your body may give up or give in.

Exercise: Identify 3 activities you did as a child that you loved, that brought out your own joy. If you still haven't found something you love that keeps you active, check this out, there's a website I love called meetup.com and they have a group of people that mingle for just about every kind of activity. Now looking back on why dancing was uncomfortable for me I realize it's also because I wasn't comfortable in my own skin. How can you fit in if you choose too if you're uncomfortable? Years later, many hours in personal development seminars, retreats, classes, coaches, and mentors, I finally feel comfortable in my approximately 200-pound *curvalicious* body. It took a lot of work and effort; however, it was completely worth it because when I'm on the dance floor, I bring sexy back like it's nobody's business, I'm just saying.

Another exercise for you: commit to taking a fun exercise and integrating this into your daily life for the next 30 days, for 30 minutes a day in childlike-joyful movement and notice how you feel and how everything changes. I would be really surprised if you weren't happier, felt more joy, and confidence even.

Seventh Key: Living Your Purpose

I am so happy and grateful now that I am living and loving my purposeful life

Finding your purpose in life is something that takes some self-discovery, and perhaps you're still figuring out what your purpose and your legacy is. As I mentioned at the start of this chapter, your legacy is so important and ought to be the thing that leads your daily life and overall goals. In order to get to this point, apply the advice in the previous sections as well as notice what your gifts are and how you shine your light. For most of my life I found myself going through the motions, simply allowing life to unveil itself to me until I realized that I am in control of my life and how I want it to unfold.

Does this seem like a lot to swallow? Well perhaps once you read this next part of my story, this concept will seem more fathomable. Just months ago, after undergoing steroid injections due to a fall, I had a severe reaction and found myself in the ER. I wasn't sure exactly how I got there; however, I do recall days leading up to the ER where I wasn't quite myself and my friends and family described me as delusional. I don't remember everything that happened once I got to the hospital however, I do vividly remember just a few hours after arriving to the ER. I heard a voice ask me one of the most powerful questions ever asked to me, *"Do you want to give up or do you want to fight?"*

Moments later I answered the question by leaving my bed, walking forward, and pleading for help. I was quickly transferred to the main hospital to undergo tests. No one knew what was wrong with me; there were theories that I was psychotic, or possibly had Meningitis (from the steroid injections like most on the East coast at the time). For two days I was in the light, fighting for my life while I underwent tests. Up until this moment, I had never recalled speaking in tongues; however, I experienced something like this while I was in the light. I can only imagine what my mother and friend visiting me thought. My mom probably thought her precious daughter was going crazy.

Later she shared with me that as they were taking me for my spinal tap, I *"looked like I did the day I was born, like a helpless baby."* Wow! Thankfully, word had spread to my friends, family, community, and many angels who were praying for me because I know that their healing prayers and my will to continue to live are what brought me out. I was finally released from the hospital with a treatable diagnosis that led to several months of healing, physical therapy, counseling and lot of love and support to get me through this unbelievable experience. I'm still figuring out why this tragic thing happened to me however, in the meantime, I'm grateful for the second chance at life. I realize that this lifetime isn't done with me yet and there is much of my legacy to be fulfilled, so I got busy working on it and continue to do so daily.

My hope for you is that you won't get to the point in your life where you have a near-death experience to step into your destiny, true calling, and purpose. However, if that is what it takes to get you there in this lifetime, then so be it. Some things to consider: are you waking up every day with joy? Or are you going through the motions and simply surviving? How is the world becoming a better place because you are in it? How can you use these things to step into your purposeful legacy? If you're still having challenges discovering your purpose here is an exercise:

In your daily journal practice, spend ten minutes of this to time describing what brings you joy. Identify talents that when expressed bring you joy and if you were to 'monetize' these gifts, what roles might you be able to fill to create financial appreciation for your gifts. Imagine a life well lived, serving from a place of complete alignment with your natural talents and being appreciated financially for them. If this is too difficult for you, think about who you know that is living a purpose that you admire or speaks to your heart and open a conversation with them; explore with them what it is like to live their purpose, etc. As you begin to embrace these tools and move forward into your true purpose, be sure to discuss with a coach/mentor to guide you and keep you on track.

Eight Key: Contribution

I am so happy and grateful now that I contribute and support my communities with love and joy.

Most people look at things and ask the question: "What is in it for me?" In fact, years ago when I was first considering writing my first book, a successful author said to me, *"Laura, no one really cares about your story; however, if you create a how-to book and incorporate your story into it, than that will have an impact and sell."* Well, that's my goal here within this book and a huge part of my contribution is volunteering and giving back. During my Reign as *Ms. Plus America,* we were required to volunteer as part of our platform and duties. Once I felt the reward that giving back had, I loved it. I've since had the fortune of working with dozens of successful coaches, mentors, entrepreneurs, authors, speakers, and artists as a volunteer. I was there to serve; however, the rewards I received from my time investment are priceless. Think about some amazing people who have the life and lifestyle you want, is there an opportunity to volunteer for them or be mentored by them? If you don't have the abundance right now to invest in a coach perhaps this is a way you could continue to grow, evolve, and develop into living your purposeful blissful life. I am fortunate to get to judge national pageants, and it's a joy to hear these young ladies talk about their great experiences volunteering at such a young age. It truly gives me chills to hear their stories and how it has changed their life for the better. I wish I knew how important volunteering is at a younger age; however, I am thankful that giving back is a large part of my life's balance now. When you can step back and come from a place of service to others, to yourself and to our planet, even more doors can open for you. In the place of giving comes much abundance.

Another aspect of contribution that is a gift is once you realize how much you really have and all the blessings in your life. When you take time to work with organizations of people that are less fortunate than yourself, it can really put things into perspective and show how abundant your life truly is, and for this you will be grateful. Compassion is a wonderful quality that can come from volunteering for others, and I now am challenging you to take on an opportunity to give back and see how things possibly shift in your life.

Exercise: Identify an area or group of people that you can volunteer at least 1 hour this month to. Where is there need and where can you serve? Where can your talents assist something so much grander in the world? I'm excited to hear about your stories of love and contribution so please visit my site and share.

Ninth Key: Balance

I am so happy and grateful for my perfectly balanced blissful life that I love.

Balance is an important part of peacefully living the blissful life you love. You may feel your life is Feng shui or in balance; however, are each a part (spiritual, physical, emotional, wealth/prosperity) of your life at a perfect 10? After releasing a large amount of weight, I had to shift and learn to enjoy the things I love in moderation. This is a big part of my motto, all things in moderation with a few exceptions. The one area that moderation doesn't need to really apply is in love.

For so many years I was doing it backwards; love in moderation and many things (like chocolate) in excess leading to an out of control and unbalanced life.

My hope for you is that you will take a hold of these tools and incorporate them into your life so that you can stay healthy and live a beautiful and balanced life. In looking at each part of balance, what are the scores you come up with yourself? The goal is a 10 for each area; however, I realize this may be a work in progress for you. For many people they have great wealth/prosperity in their life with little time to enjoy it which can lead to a detriment in the other areas of their life like their relationships (emotional aspect). While others may have great health towards their physical aspect however, there is little peace and relaxation in their life, which negatively affects their spiritual balance aspect. All of these elements are equally important and trust me this balance is something I strive for and continue to work on every moment; it's part of the journey. Looking around at the lifestyle you have, the relationships in your life, your health, and overall piece of mind are a reflection on how you are (or are not) balanced in life.

Exercise: Take out a piece of paper and put a square in the middle and on each side of it write the following: spiritual at the top, emotional at the bottom, physical on the right-hand side, wealth/prosperity on the left-hand side. Spiritual represents your connection with God. Emotional represents relationship with self, others, family, and friends. Physical represents health, nutrition, and exercise. Wealth/prosperity represents bank account, investments, value exchange, relationship with money and career. On a scale 1-10 (10 being the highest possible), put a number for each area that represents your relationship in each one of these areas. Now, is each area a 10? If not, then why? Journal for ten minutes to explore ways you could make the number you have written one point higher towards the 10 mark. What are some ways that you could improve each of these areas and the relationship you have in that area of your life?

Tenth Key: Gratitude

I am so happy and grateful now that I live life from a loving, grateful heart.

Truly focusing on and appreciating all the things you are grateful for what brings more of these blessings to you. It may seem silly; however, what you focus on becomes evident in your life. The more gratitude you have for abundance, more will come. The more gratitude you have for the love for yourself and your life, the more love comes to you in everything you do and experience. Remember earlier when I spoke about how you start your day? Here's an exercise for you to start each morning (meditation, prayer, etc.): spend five minutes in gratitude and set your intention throughout the day from a place of what you are grateful for. Repeat these affirmations, *"I am so happy and grateful now that I am in perfect health. I am so happy and grateful now for my loving and dynamic relationships."* Think about the four aspects of balance and create your own: *"I am so happy and grateful now that... (FILL IN BLANK)."*

At the end of the day, journal how things may have shifted for you, and how you are grateful for what happened throughout that day.

Another element of showing your appreciation and gratitude is by simply smiling and saying thank you. This may seem so simple however a smile and a heart-felt thank you can completely change a person's attitude and a situation.

Now that I have shared all these empowering tools with you, I'm excited for you to implement these practices. Now it is time for you to take some action! It may feel a little overwhelming as I shared a lot of information as well as my stories; however, I'm here to support you. Although your journey is unique to you, you're not alone and there is love all around you to guide you through this wonderful path of self-love. It's a little selfish of me, I suppose, because the more empowered people in the world that come from a place of love and gratitude, the better world we all live in. I look forward to hearing from you and how I can further serve and support you on your journey so please reach out to me. Many blessings toward your prosperity, success and fulfilling your blissful loving purpose on your journey towards self-love.

CHAPTER REFLECTION:

1. Which key will you apply to your life?

2. How will you apply the key?

3. How will you measure your success?

Write down your responses to the above reflection in the *Woman of Purpose, Power and Passion Companion Journal*; and apply the additional keys to your life as well. Make sure that you reward yourself for goals attained.

WOMAN OF
PURPOSE, POWER
AND PASSION

Bring the plans, dreams, and visions that God has placed in your heart into fulfillment, by keeping a record to reflect and to ACT upon.

COMPANION JOURNAL

SCAN TO BUY

ISBN#: 9781941580004

BOOK REVIEWS

If this book has been a blessing to you, please scan the QR Code below to post a review on Amazon or write a review where you purchased this book.

SCAN TO BUY

Thank you for taking the time to post a review!

ADDITIONAL EDITIONS

5-Star Reviews

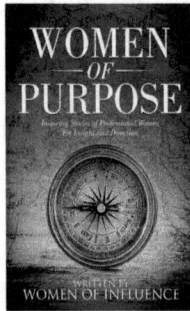

ISBN#: 9781941580424

ISBN#: 9781941580462

HigginsPublishing.com

RECOMMENDED READ

The Journey in Between Helps You Navigate Mid-Life During Times of Loss, Grief, Fear and Transition.

The Journey in Between empty nesters book by Eileen Deadwiler – Helps You Navigate the Terrain in Between Life's Moments by Applying Biblical Text and Acknowledging God's Presence.

The Journey in Between mid-life book is perfect for you if you find yourself stuck between life's moments. This book helps you cope with hard choices, complete life-changing situations, adversity, grief and loss, or fear. Insights within *The Journey in Between* book offers empathetic insights into how you can find comfort and compassion when you open your heart to God's lessons and words.

When life seems complex, complicated, and challenging to face the hurdles or in times of uncertainty, *The Journey in Between* book offers solutions. This mid-life book for women and men is what you need to learn that every step you take forward is progress.

SCAN TO BUY

ISBN#: 9781941580226 PB
ISBN#: 9781941580233 HB

INDEX